CIRENCESTER:

The Development and Buildings of a
Cotswold Town

Cirencester:
the Development
and Buildings of a
Cotswold Town

Richard Reece

&

Christopher Catling

British Archaeological Reports 12
1975

British Archaeological Reports

122 Banbury Road, Oxford OX2 7BP, England

Details of all issues of British Archaeological Reports will be sent free of charge and without any obligation to purchase, on request from the above address.

B.A.R. 12, 1975: "Cirencester: the Development and Buildings of a Cotswold Town". © Richard Reece and Christopher Catling, 1975.

Price £1.50 ($4.00) post free.

Cheques and postal orders should be made payable to "British Archaeological Reports" and sent to the above address.

For a list of other B.A.R. publications, please see the last page.

Printed in Great Britain
by TRUEXpress Ltd Oxford

PREFACE

This report is the result of a survey which we carried out for five weeks in August and September, 1974. Before we actually started work we had found the relevant maps and obtained copies of them, and we both had the advantage of living in Cirencester. Apart from this all the work of the survey was carried out by two people working a full eight hour day, six days a week for exactly five weeks.

Financial help for materials, copies of maps, travel, and expenses during and after the actual work came from the Russell Trust, the Bristol and Gloucestershire Archaeological Society and the Cirencester Archaeological and Historical Society. The total budget was £305.

Mark Webber and Mike Weir gave us help over obtaining maps, and the Gloucestershire County Record Office and the Bingham Public Library gave us much help and access to books and records. As soon as work on the manuscript was complete Lynda Greenwood reduced a variety of illegible notes to an orderly typescript and Bob Downey prepared all our drawings for publication. Our photographs were handed over to Julian Munby and Hugh Toller who produced the prints, and Julian Munby mounted the plates. Peter Dorrell and Geoffrey Denford reduced the drawings to the correct size, and David Wilkinson produced the drawing of 51 Coxwell Street for the frontispiece.

The project has not been rationalised as part of a gradiloquent design, or undertaken as a section of a nationwide survey. It is nothing to do with any learned society or statutory body. When we were looking at the buildings, one by one, we were mistaken either for sanitary inspectors, lighting engineers, or investigators of a Royal Commission on Historical Monuments. It is sad that no one assumed what was in fact the case, that we were doing the survey because we wanted to. This has all been better said before by Samuel Rudder in the preface to the second edition of his History of Cirencester (Cirencester 1800) and we let him speak for us:

"In a multifarious undertaking, embracing so many subjects, perfection is not to be expected; but we can truly say, that nothing is wilfully misrepresented; and if at any time we should be found tripping, the candid reader will be mindful that to err is the common failing of human nature, from which no mortal is exempt.

There seems to be no great occasion to declare our motives to publication; but since others have done so we have no objection to follow their example. Let it suffice, then, to say that having collected materials, and arranged them in some order for our own amusement, we feel a certain gratification in communicating to others the information which has

given us some pleasure in collecting; and that
gratification will be further heightened, in
proportion as the reader may be rationally enter-
tained, and as our endeavours may find a favourable
reception.

January 16th, 1800"

To all our friends and colleagues, named and un-named
who have helped us so willingly and speedily we give our
best thanks, and hope that they find it worthwhile.

Cirencester, November 1974.

CONTENTS

LIST OF ILLUSTRATIONS

Page

FIGURES

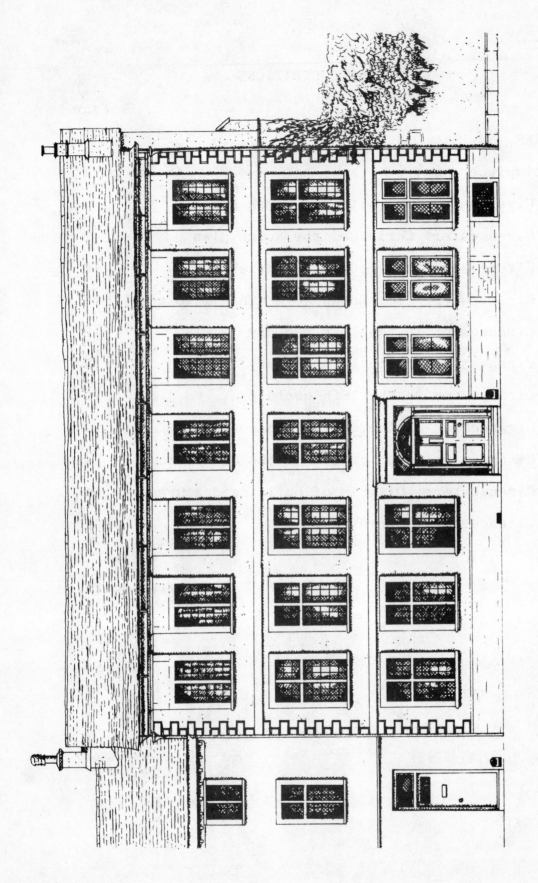

FRONTISPIECE: 51, Coxwell Street. Drawn by: D. Wilkinson.

INTRODUCTION

This is a detailed study of one aspect of the growth
and development of a small modern market town. This market
town, Cirencester, is now a community of some ten to twenty
thousand people depending where you draw the boundaries,
and which villages you take as forming a part of the whole.
It lies in a south east corner of Gloucestershire on the
dip slope of the Cotswold hills with the county boundary
with Wiltshire a few miles to the south and east.

Roman Cirencester, Corinium Dobunnorum, was a very much
more important town ranking always as a Civitas capital,
and, at times as the capital of a Roman Province. Second
only in defended area to London it bears comparison with any
other city in Roman Britain and, in the fourth century, has
few competitors in size and sophistication north of the
Alps. The title Civitas capital is interesting for it
compares well with the position of Cirencester in post-
Roman times.

At the Roman conquest the country was divided up into
tribal groupings for ease of government, tax collection,
and general control. The tribe in this part of the country,
the Dobunni, had a centre at Bagendon; the Roman re-organisation moved this centre to Cirencester. A large town was
marked out to act as the centre of a tribal area whose
extent is not known in detail but which seems to stretch
west, over the Severn into the Forest of Dean and Hereford-
shire, north into Worcestershire, east into Oxfordshire
and Berkshire, and south into Wiltshire and towards Bath.
This was the Civitas of the Dobunni and Corinium was its
centre.

After the end of the Roman administration we know little
of the status of the town. It is recorded fairly early in
the Saxon period as a Villa Regalis, or Royal Manor or
town, but it could not compete with the county town at
Gloucester, the seat of the Bishopric at Worcester, or the
growing towns of Oxford and Bristol. Cirencester had
dwarfed all these towns in the Roman period; in the early
middle ages each one of these towns had its own sphere of
influence so that the medieval Civitas, or area of control
of Cirencester was much smaller than the Roman Civitas.

At Domesday survey Cirencester was the only market in
this Cotswold area, and the establishment of a re-endowed
and later mitred Abbey ensured that the town kept pace
with the ring of competitors grouped around it. By the end
of the sixteenth century the town was a flourishing market
town in the modern sense, of little interest to any but its
inhabitants. They, in turn, took little part or interest
in the wider events elsewhere, and it is in this atmosphere
that the town has emerged as capital of the Cotswolds. For
the tourist the town is a picturesque centre of a pictures-

que area. For the inhabitants of the modern Civitas it
is a place to visit once or twice a week, by irregular bus
service, to shop, to pay bills, to find services and
advice, to work, or to go to school.

It is against this background that our survey of
standing buildings must be seen. The survey is material
in that it concentrates on physical evidence in the field.
Much more could have been done with historical sources such
as the cartularies of the Abbey and smaller documents such
as the Lady Chapel Register of 1460. These have, for the
moment, been left on one side; they are relatively safe
and available for future study. This also applies to the
great mass of legal material in the County Record Office.

As far as possible we have kept to commonly accepted
terms when describing buildings, and for this, as for so
many other things, Mr. Verey's Buildings of Gloucestershire
has been invaluable. Only in one case have we <u>knowingly</u>
invented a new term - the Cecily Hill lintel. This is
shorthand for a flat lintel which forms the head of a
rectangular window or door, made up of stone voussoirs
whose upper and lower ends form two parallel lines, but
whose upper ends, as in all voussoirs, are thicker than
their lower ends. As the earliest dated example occurs
at 11-15 Cecily Hill, and that road shows many other
examples of such lintels, we have supplied a short name
for a common feature which has otherwise found only long
descriptive titles.

A critical and select bibliography will be found in
the section on 'Sources' pp 35 to 38.

THE EARLY BACKGROUND - FROM FOUNDATION TO THE REFORMATION

The study of Cirencester, at any stage in its development, needs an understanding of the phases which have gone before. There is only one point at which we may be reasonably certain that there is no earlier phase, and that is the Roman fort which kept a watchful eye on the Dobunni at Bagendon, and its successor, the Civitas capital, Corinium Dobunnorum (1).

Sometime shortly after the birth of Christ the Dobunni seem to have made a settlement at Bagendon which grew into a tribal capital consisting of an area of acres defended by man-made ditches and natural swamps, rivers and woodland. At the Roman conquest of AD 43 a part of a tribe recorded as Bodunni sent a surrender to the Roman forces and it seems likely that these people were in fact the Dobunni of Bagendon (2). If this is true it means that when the Roman forces moved swiftly through the south and east of Britain subduing the tribes who caused trouble, and ensuring the co-operation of the less warlike, a small fort at the point at which the Whiteway forded the river Churn was all that was needed to secure the tribal territory while the armies marched on, north and west.

Somewhere around AD 75 the fort was forgotten, the Britons were encouraged to become Romanized, and the archaeological record joins the Roman historian Tacitus (3) who tells us that one of the spearheads of Romanization was the laying out of towns and the planning of the great public buildings such as the central basilica with its attendant Forum to serve as civic centre and shopping precinct. The erection of such a large building and courtyard automatically determined the layout of the rest of the town, for the forum-basilica unit was usually one square, or insula, of a chess board plan. Once the streets had been lined up on the sides of the rectangular market place four main lines in the town were set, and other streets and building blocks tended to follow both dimensions and alignments.

Fig. 1a suggests that the fort was founded where the meandering river Churn cut the Whiteway. Neither the course of the river nor the age of the Whiteway are known, but the river presumably flowed down the lowest part of the valley, the path of least resistance, and the Whiteway is one non-Roman (that is, non-geometrically aligned) trackway which is needed by villas, settlements, and later developments to be at least Roman in date, and probably earlier. Fig. 1b suggests the alignments of the roads in the Roman period. While there is little doubt about their paths as they approach the town site, we know very little of their course as they actually join the town.

The Whiteway is shown in its presumed early course before it was diverted by the Abbey and the later Abbey

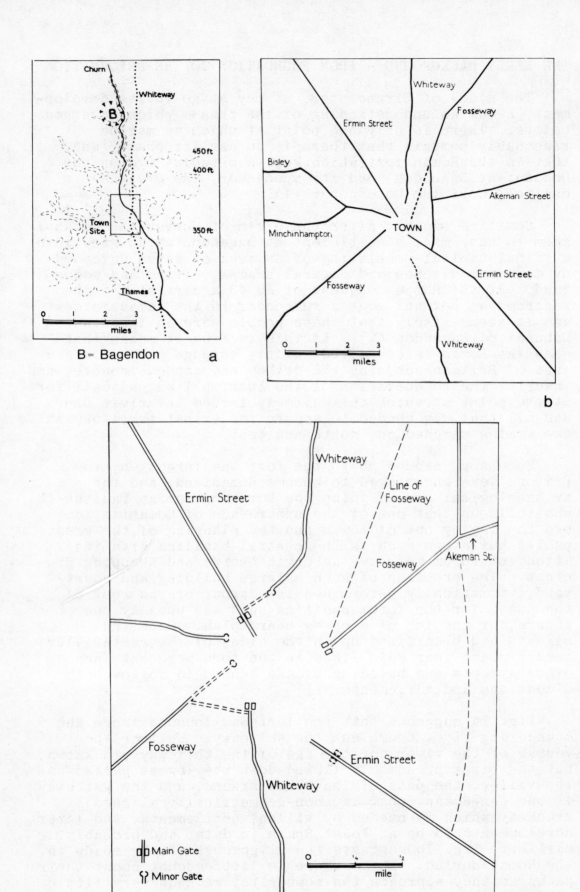

B = Bagendon   a

b

Whiteway

Line of
Fosseway

Ermin Street

Fosseway   Akeman St.

Akeman St.

Fosseway

Whiteway

Ermin Street

▯◻ Main Gate

ᕲᶜ Minor Gate

Fig. 1   c

Cirencester: the site and Roman roads

Estate, the Canal and the Railway. The Fosseway makes
several changes of direction as it approaches the town
site from the north-east; the final alignment takes it
to a junction with Akeman Street and thence it forms what
has been taken to be a Roman by-pass leading to Ermin
Street at Preston toll-bar. If the final re-alignment is
ignored, as in the dotted line, the approaching road can
be made to aim satisfactorily for the Verulamium gate of
the town. No alignment of Akeman Street makes very good
sense as it comes in from the east, and this point
together with the fact that this is the only Roman road
to be severely dislocated in its path out of the town in
later times, might suggest that this is a later, subsidiary
Roman road of limited use. The alignment of Ermin Street,
approaching from the south-east, carries on inside the
later town boundary for a short way and this alignment
seems to be ancient. It seems very reasonable to suggest
that it is only inside the walls that the Roman road bent
to conform to the street grid. The Whiteway, leaving the
town almost due south, has perhaps not so far been given
its due, for even Beecham (4) in pointing the strange
alignment of a possible "postern" gate near the amphitheatre, does not connect it with the Whiteway. This kink
in the town wall, through which the Roman street aligned
on the modern Lewis Lane is assumed to have extended to
the amphitheatre, has been removed from recent plans of
the Roman town. It is due for reinstatement after the
observation of recent trenching which again picked up
solid Roman walling and possible gateway on just this skew
angle which seems to make so little sense. Here perhaps
we have a Corinian example of early building, e.g. the
site of a gate, being set on an alignment, the Whiteway,
which was later to become far less important as new
patterns of movement grew up.

So far we have looked at the roads from north to south
moving clockwise round the town; the second half of the
road system poses more problems, not because we have
conflicting knowledge, but too little knowledge. The main
ancient route leaving the town to the south-west is the
Fosseway on its way to Bath. From its present junction
with the Stroud Road and Chesterton Lane, to its dislocation at Jacament's Bottom there is no reason to doubt the
course of the Roman road. Presumably medieval Tetbury
exerted a greater attraction than a direct route to Bath
so that there is little problem in explaining the large
break in use of the Fosseway between Cirencester and Bath.
Nearer to the town the lack of knowledge becomes limiting
for not only is there a complete absence of any real
evidence for a gate at the south-west end of Castle Street,
but there is no sure evidence that any road ran into the
town here. Evidence from excavations near the amphitheatre
and observations made when the new hospital at The Querns
was being constructed strongly suggest that the main road
might swing across from the top of the Tetbury Road hill
to enter at the Whiteway gate. A path no doubt led

directly down the hill to a small postern gate to the south of the Mansion.

The laying out of the park in the early 18th century closed two roads which presumably started from Cecily Hill. On the plan of 1793 Cecily Hill is marked 'from Hampton'. This must represent the road crossing the present park, joining at some point with the present Stroud Road, and continuing over the common to Minchinhampton. The other road from Cecily Hill is generally held to have led from the Barton to the Ewe Pens and thence to Park Corner and Bisley. The new Stroud Road opened by Lord Bathurst skirts the Deerpark and Oakley Wood and in doing so emphasises the Tetbury Road exit from the town; the route to Bisley and Sapperton had to go through Stratton and Daglingworth. Finally Ermin Street goes out to Gloucester almost on its original alignment from the Church tower, where it was recently checked in a small exploratory excavation, over a minor dislocation at the Gloucester Street bridge, up a spur of high land, to pass over the scarp to the nearby Colonia. This diverse information can be forced into a single statement in fig. 1c which, it must be remembered, contains much that is uncertain if not tendentious.

The Town

Fig. 1c shows one thing both clearly and without any doubt; the roads coming into the town, or leading out, give very little help in establishing the Roman street plan. This strongly suggests that the planning of the town was a reasonably late feature only put into practice when the surrounding roads, and perhaps some of the gates, were firmly established. This fits in with what we know of the chronology of the town, the fort, the defences and the gates. The road system connecting the military, and presumably civil, administration in or near the fort with the landowners and villagers scattered round the territory of the Dobunni, grew up in the thirty years between the conquest and the army evacuation. Beyond the purely local horizon some roads must have been of official construction to join the Dobunni to neighbouring settlements like the camp, and later Colonia, at Gloucester, through the capital of the Atrebates at Silchester, to London, through Oxford-shire to Verulamium, and up the Fosseway eventually to Lincoln. We suggest that the Whiteway needs more prominence in the early period than has formerly been allowed to it, even to the extent of allowing it a major gateway to the town. But the alignments of the roads can have given little help to the planners for there is scarcely a near right angle between any two approaching roads.

At some time after the abandonment of the fort a boundary was drawn, and whatever the reasons for taking the line that they did, the point needs to be made that the planners enclosed an area far larger than they could reasonably

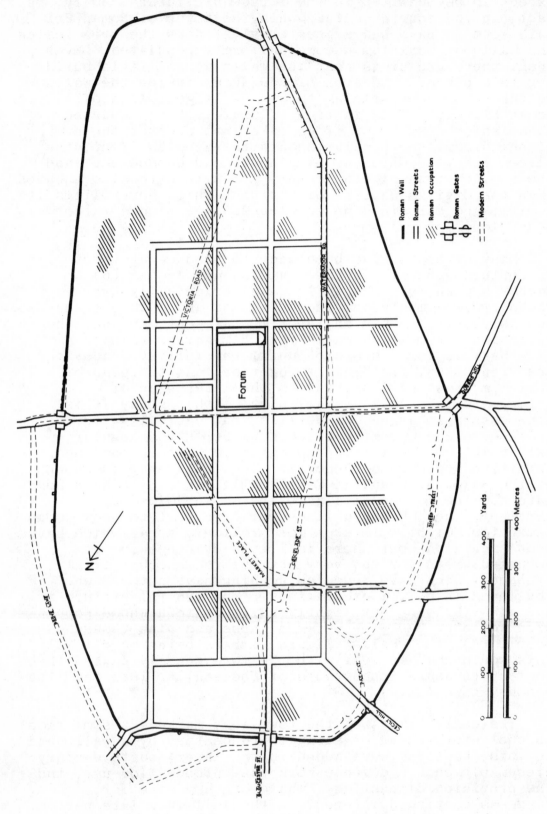

Fig. 2

Cirencester: Corinium, the Roman plan

expect to be built up in the forseeable future. Only, in fact, in the fourth century when the towns of Roman Britain seem to have had a great revival does the area inside the walls of Corinium become uniformly populated. Even then, there are areas near the walls where little building took place. The area of 240 acres inside the walls is taken to make Corinium the second largest town of Roman Britain. This is true if what is being counted is defended area. But if we take into account the number of buildings, the population and the area built up, then places like the Coloniae of Lincoln and Gloucester, and the smaller town of Winchester, all with extensive suburbs, then the Civitas capital of Corinium which never fills its limits, and certainly never exceeds them, looks rather undeveloped.

Many attempts have been made to produce a street plan of Corinium, notably by Beecham (5) and Wacher (6). Wacher's plan, brought up to date periodically by MacWhirr (7), must form the basis for any future discussions, but as yet it is only an interim statement, so that the variations from it shown in fig. 2 might be allowed as alternatives for discussion until the full evidence, and the final plan, are brought together. As the plan of Corinium, however important to the later plan of Cirencester, is only a small part of this study it is unnecessary to argue out details, but basically fig. 2 represents a compromise between Wacher's rectangular extrapolation of his archaeological evidence, and the intuitive approach of Beecham. Thus a gateway is shown at the Saxon Arch and at Cecily Hill, and the London Road gate and the Querns Hill gate are shown joined by a straight line. Hatched lines which purport to show Roman occupation might well show more reliably areas which have been excavated, but there is little evidence for un-occupied areas for the very obvious reason that trial trenches which have revealed nothing have never been developed into full excavations. The general picture is one of a thriving but lightly built up town whose population would probably be between three and nine thousand people (8), the smaller figure perhaps being more likely. This would compare well with the more densely packed three to four thousand inhabitants of the smaller 16th and 17th century town (9).

The early limits of the town were marked at some time in the later second or early third century by a wall, and to this, bastions were added in the later fourth century. Presumably such a defence work was intended for use, and the provision of bastions, whatever they were for, suggests continued interest in the wall in a late period. Such length of walling could presumably never have been defended over its whole extent but must have been intended to ward off a raid, rather than a seige, with a small force guarding gateways and towers. A small force would need to be experienced to be of any use so that we almost

certainly have to think of a well trained home guard, or
a small garrison of regular soldiers, in later Corinium.
Money flows into the town in undiminished bulk, to judge
from the coins found, up until the time around AD 402 when
the mints of Gaul ceased production of copper coins. One
reason for this continued supply of coin may well have
been troops needing regular wages and small change; the
wages would have been gold, the small change, copper.

About the end of Corinium we know very little. The
forum contained very little debris when excavated, and the
absence of late coins led Wacher to suggest that the forum
was kept clean until no coins were available to be lost
(10). This seems a perfectly acceptable idea, and, if
correct, it would extend the life of the central meeting
place of the town up to about AD 420. No site yet
excavated has produced any evidence of destruction; the
rule seems to be gentle decay with the ruins often showing
rubble areas and patches, like pathways and farmyards. As
the provincial administration ground to a halt early in
the fifth century, and the tribal administration became
very much simpler in that there was now no Empire with
whom to connect, and no Imperial taxes or levies to be
met, the population of Corinium must have declined. The
one class of citizen who had no reason to move was the
farmer who attended to his fields and animals around the
town from a town house indistinguishable from a country
farm (11), and it may be that the population of fifth
century Corinium was no more than a collection of farming
families. The church no doubt continued, a titular chief
or king continued, but few buildings needed to be kept up
for human occupation. As the farms were divided up, or
joined together, were ruined, or rebuilt in a different
spot, the pattern of the Roman town was almost erased and
Cirencester began.

Fig. 3 shows the medieval borough which succeeded the
Roman town with a ring of tythings around it. If a set
of unsupported assertions may be admitted here then we
can hint that future work will argue in detail a case for
taking the borough as the remains of the property of the
descendant of the head of the Roman Civitas, and the three
surrounding tythings as heirs to three or four late Roman
farmsteads based in or near the late Roman town. Barton
Tything is therefore suggested as the descendant of the
farm of the Barton Roman Villa (12), Chesterton Tything is
controlled by the manor and a farm, the manor perhaps
descending from a Roman town house, and two halves of
Sperringate Tything, divided by the Fosse Way, centre on
the Golden Farm, now in Beeches Road, and Whiteway farm.
Fig. 3 includes four sites in Sperringate Tything which
may be relevant to this theory: i) an early Iron Age farmstead, as yet only known from aerial photographs and trial
trenches, ii) an early Roman farmstead discovered during
the construction of the ring-road in 1974, iii) the
Beeches Road Roman farmhouse (13) and iv) the present

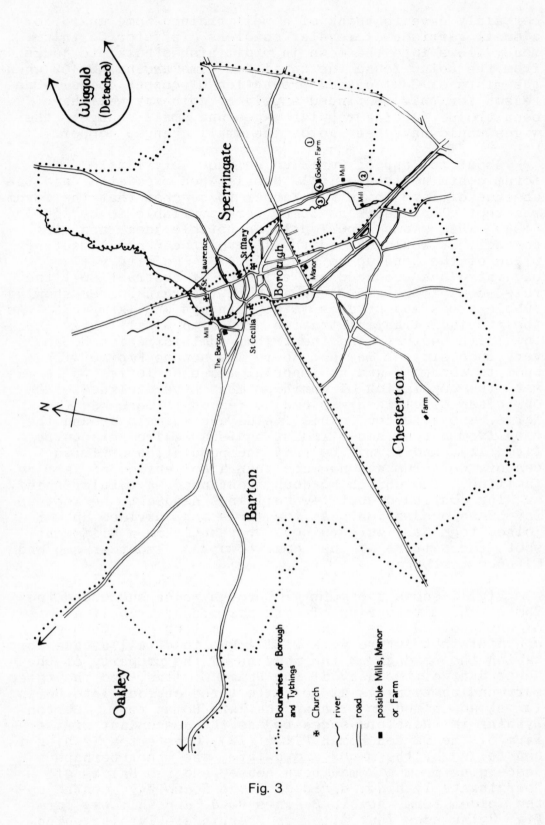

Fig. 3

Cirencester: the mediaeval Parish

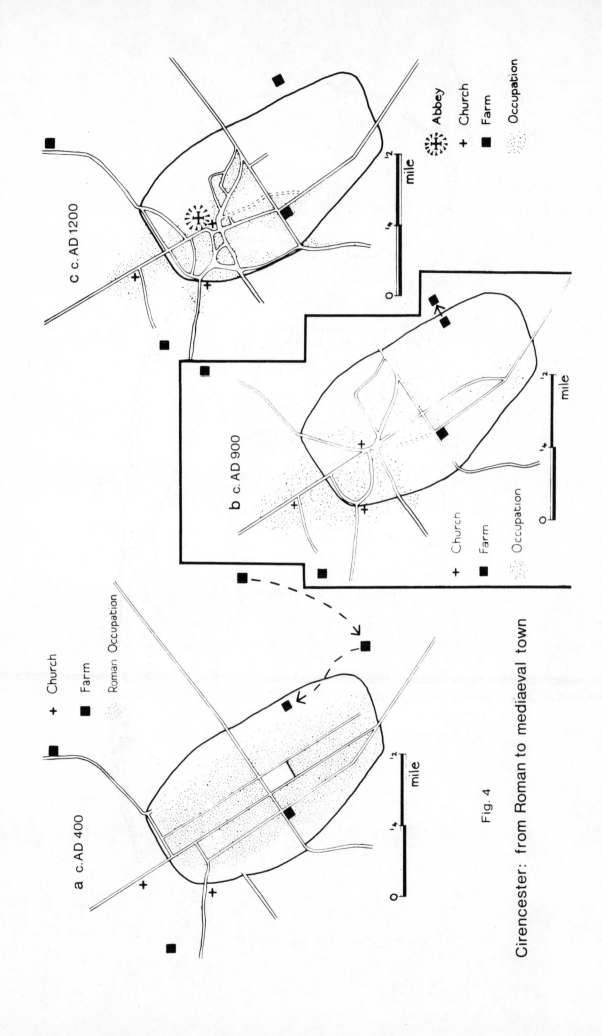

a c. AD 400

+ Church
■ Farm
⠿ Roman Occupation

0 ¼ ½ mile

b c. AD 900

+ Church
■ Farm
⠿ Occupation

0 ¼ ½ mile

C c. AD 1200

✻ Abbey
+ Church
■ Farm
⠿ Occupation

0 ¼ ½ mile

Fig. 4

Cirencester: from Roman to mediaeval town

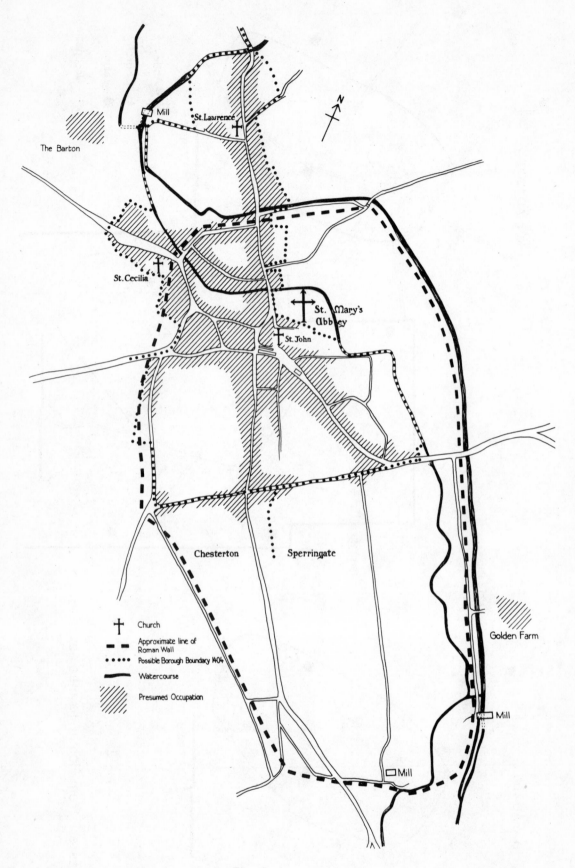

Fig. 5

Cirencester in the 15th C.

Golden Farm (see Beeches Road in list and plate II). A
set of three outline diagrams given in fig. 4 puts these
suggestions in visual form.

Fig. 5 concentrates on the medieval borough and shows
the boundary established in 1404 (14). When the borough
boundary is compared with the boundary formed by the
Roman wall it is easily seen that a strong shift has taken
place to the north west. Two institutions which lie in
the borough, but not in the Roman town are the churches of
St. Cecilia and St. Lawrence. Both these churches were in
decline by the Reformation when they were thought scarcely
worth notice (15). It is for this reason that they will
be found on fig. 4a marked as late Roman cemetery churches.
Such suggestions may seem of the highest unreliability, but
a late Roman origin is far simpler as an explanation for
these churches than any suggestion based on events in the
early Saxon period, completely devoid of historical
references and parallels.

One suggestion for the north-west shift may therefore
be stated as a religious shift. Once the centre of gravity
has moved north, the roads, in a lightly populated settlement of shack smallholdings make direct for their object,
the centre of activity. The new church was placed near
the main north-west to south-east road of Ermin Street with
scant regard for the buildings which preceded it.
Foundation trenches were dug into the remains of Roman
buildings, and these were filled with building stone, much
carved decoration, and architectural moulding to form a
firm basis for the walls of the church (16). Whenever
this operation took place, whether under St. Wilfred
during his years of exile in the seventh century, or under
St. Aldwyn in the ninth, Roman buildings were being
demolished and cleared away at a considerable rate, and if
the process continued for any length of time the Roman town
would soon have presented a uniform flat vista. By the mid
twelfth century a silver penny of John in a robbing trench
shows that the builders of the Abbey were having to dig
below ground level for their stone, an unnecessary labour
in the presence of extensive ruins (17).

The main north-east to south-west road seems to have
continued through the town from one gate to another, but
most of the other streets came from a Roman gate direct
to the centre; one road from the Whiteway and the
Spittlegate was later diverted by the Abbey, one from
Cecily Hill became Park Street and Black Jack Street,
Castle Street continued the Tetbury Road into the centre,
and Chipping Street (Dyer Street) led traffic from the
London Road gate direct to the Market place. In spite of
the continuance of Ermin Street south-east from the new
church the Roman road from the south-east gate to
Chesterton Manor gradually extended on a non-Roman line
towards the Market place to form the present Cricklade
Street. The old line lingered on to be shown by Kip as a
trackway, and to give part of the boundary between

Sperringate and Chesterton tythings.

With the foundation of the Abbey a new parish church had to be built for the town, and the church of St. John rose very near to the line of Ermin Street. The Abbey kept travellers away from their domain and the open space to the north-east of the town, still enjoyed today, was marked out. The parish church prospered, was extended, and finally cut Ermin Street by using it as foundation for its tower: consequently the south-east portion of the Roman line declined to Kip's trackway and the modern property boundaries, and the West Market Place was formed. Oakley Cottage, later Allen Bathurst's new park hemmed in the town to the west, and the Abbey Estate to the east; Gloucester Street was already spread well out to the north-west, so that when the town came to grow expansion had to be to the south-east. By about 1921 the town had just about regained its Roman shape and size; it is with the buildings of the post-medieval town and its expansion that the rest of this study is concerned.

References

1. J.S. Wacher, Ant.J., 1962, XLII, 1-14.
2. E.M. Clifford, Bagendon - a Belgic Oppidum, Cambridge, 1961, 56-74.
3. Tacitus, Agricola, 21.
4. Beecham, History of Cirencester, 1886, 249.
5. Beecham, History of Cirencester, 1886, facing 250.
6. J.S. Wacher, Ant.J., 1963, XLIII, 17.
7. A.D. MacWhirr, Ant.J., 1969, XLIX, 223.
8. S.S. Frere, Britannia (2nd ed.), London 1974, 296-7.
9. Beecham, History of Cirencester, 1886, 194.
10. J.S. Wacher, Ant.J., 1964, XLIV, 14.
11. Current Archaeology, 42, 216-9.
12. Buckman and Newmarch, Remains of Roman Art, London, 1850, 32-4.
13. Current Archaeology, 42, 216-9.
14. Beecham, History of Cirencester, 1886, 155-7.
15. Beecham, History of Cirencester, 1886, 90-1.
16. P.D.C. Brown and A.D. MacWhirr, Ant.J., 1967, XLVII, 195-7.
17. R. Reece, Trans. Bristol and Glos. Arch. Soc., 75, 1956, 203-4.

Whether the reformation, including the dissolution of the monasteries, made a great difference to the life of the man in the street of Cirencester may be doubted. The Royal Commissioners arrived at the Abbey at noon on December 19th, 1539 (1), and by the end of the week matters had been settled, so far as we know amicably, pensions had been dispensed, and Roger Basing, one of the king's wine merchants had been made responsible for the safe keeping of the assets, and was eventually charged with the demolition of the Abbey and its buildings. The demolition clause included in the lease of the site to Basing on May 11th, 1540 is part of the usual language of such leases, and, provided the king received the lead from the roof, the bells, and the smaller valuables there is no need to assume that the buildings were demolished speedily. In this case, however, most of the stone seems to have been bought by two local people, Robert Strange and Sir Anthony Hungerford, and since they complained to the Court of Augmentations that they were being obstructed in their demolition and stone carrying, things must have moved fairly quickly (1).

The removal of St. Mary's Abbey made little difference to the growth of the town, for the lands passed to Richard Master who built the first Abbey House a little to the west of the former cloisters, and the walls of the Abbey Estate blocked growth to the north-east just as effectively as the monastic community had done. This was, with hind-sight, no bad thing, for it explains the large open area, now belonging to the town, which reaches to within yards of the Market Place. It might have been a little less expensive if the town had had the forethought to acquire the land in 1539 for Dr. Master only paid £59.16s.3d. for his whole estate (1).

The later 16th century seems to have marked a change from extensive use of timber to a greater use of stone, if the surviving buildings are a representative sample of what was built before 1600. The physical structure of the Abbey contributed little or nothing to the new stone buildings for not only was the stone sold to be carted away, but in terms of re-usable material it would have built very little. This change to stone is either a local fashion, or may be a reflection of the opening up of quarries on Abbey land which was previously inaccessible. Apart from Monmouth House, Thomas Street, and some of the timber framed buildings we know very little of the aspect of the town through the early 17th century, and it is not until the dated buildings of Coxwell Street and Gloucester Street begin to appear later in the century that we catch glimpses of the post-medieval town. Prints showing Butter Row and Shoe Lane, the narrow streets removed from the centre of the Market Place in 1826, show a preponderance of half-timbered buildings, and those buildings which are recognisably of stone usually belong to the styles of the 1670's and later (2).

The earliest view of the town is that by J. Kip, a
Dutchman who was commissioned by Sir Robert Atkyns to
provide illustrations for his monumental work "The Ancient
and Present State of Gloucestershire". These copper plates
were mainly of country homes, sometimes with a small town
or village in the distance, but views of Cirencester and
Gloucester are published entire. The inclusion of the
County town with its cathedral is easily understood, but
it is less obvious why Kip chose to draw the whole of
Cirencester rather than just the house of Allen Bathurst,
whose seat the caption proclaims this to be. It is
important to suggest his reasons because there are certain
major inaccuracies in the drawing which may be explained if
we can understand Kip's artistic approach to the town.

The two great Estates of the Abbey and Oakley had forced
the town to grow into two triangles their apexes meeting at
the Parish Church. This pattern may have appealed to the
draughtsman, and having decided to put part of the town into
his picture, it certainly provided a challenge. Unless he
was going to be completely inaccurate it is difficult to
see how he could have avoided portraying part of the town
for the front of Oakley Grove faces the town, and any use
of Kip's favourite perspective would inevitably lead to
houses in the foreground.

The next decision was the exact line which the view was
to take; it must neither obscure Oakley Grove, nor relegate
it to a position of secondary importance. Chief among
difficult features was the parish church which, if made the
focal point of the picture, would totally obscure the house.
The church must be set to one side, and he therefore had
the choice of views of the town to the north or south of
the church. If he had chosen a view to the north of the
church the major building would have been the Abbey House
in the centre of the picture, and this was already to
appear in a separate engraving. The south view was therefore chosen with the advantage of relegating the Abbey
House to a less imposing position and allowing the Market
Place, suitably adjusted, to form an impressive approach
straight through the town to the chosen building. This
perhaps gives some of the reasoning behind the composition
of the picture which shows the Bathurst home as an imposing
building at the head of a prosperous market town, the wings
of the Jacobean mansion spread out to embrace the town.

Having already adjusted reality to make his picture
it might be thought that all Kip's other inaccuracies stem
from the same point. This scarcely explains the chief
blunder by which the tower of the Parish Church has been
placed above the middle of the nave instead of in its
correct position at the west end. This provides a
structure of very odd appearance possibly unparalleled
anywhere in fact; the tower of Fairford church lies at
the east end of the nave providing the traditional crossing into the choir, but it is not even this that Kip has
shown, for there is unmistakable nave roof between the
tower and the choir.

Mention of the tower allows a speculation for the one place where an accurate perspective drawing of the church could not be done is the top of the tower itself. It is presumably from there that Kip must have made outline sketches later to be turned into a finished drawing, and if his view of the church was from its tower, and from the ground level of the Market Place where it was completely surrounded by houses, then his mistake might be more easily condoned. One very odd fact is the similarity between Kip and the draughtsman of the 1793 map, who in nearly every other detail is excellent; both omit the Parish Church porch.

The left foreground of the picture makes Kip's other mistake very obvious for he has made the triangle formed by Lewis Lane, Cricklade Street and Dyer Street into a large square. To fill this large, partly non-existent space Kip has provided a rectangular formal garden in the foreground and has then spaced out the middle distance. This means that he has made a pathway which crosses this block stand out more clearly than it otherwise would. If the perspective is corrected the path would run from the King's Head to a point on Lewis Lane somewhere just west of Tower Street and it seems likely that the path represents the line of Ermin Street which Kip saw in its last period of use. Later drawings and maps show this only as a rough path, and later a property boundary.

The re-arrangement of Castle Street, Silver Street, Park Lane, and Sheep Street are best explained as artistic convention. Sheep Street had to go so that the Bathurst house could be shown at the head of a straightened out Market Place, Castle Street and Silver Street. Castle Street then bends round to the left to meet Querns Lane at the foot of Tetbury Hill. As with Lewis Lane, which Kip ran out of his picture unnecessarily, Sheep Street probably contained few imposing buildings so that there was little need to present them accurately.

With these points in mind Kip's drawing seems to be a reasonably accurate representation of Cirencester at the beginning of the 18th century. The major buildings are given individual treatment which in some cases can be checked against surviving facades, though smaller buildings are mainly in stylised form. Gloucester House, Dyer Street appears as an imposing house and garden, the Ram Inn with its courtyard is in the correct place at the head of the Market Place, and Monmouth House, Thomas Street shows a plain facade with few and small windows which accords well with what survives. Inns in the Market Place and Dyer Street are marked in their correct positions by conventional inn-signs on poles and the watercourses and bridges provide few difficulties. From the drawing it has been possible to prepare a map of the town as it was in 1712 with surviving buildings marked in detail and the other buildings blocked in and stippled (fig. 6).

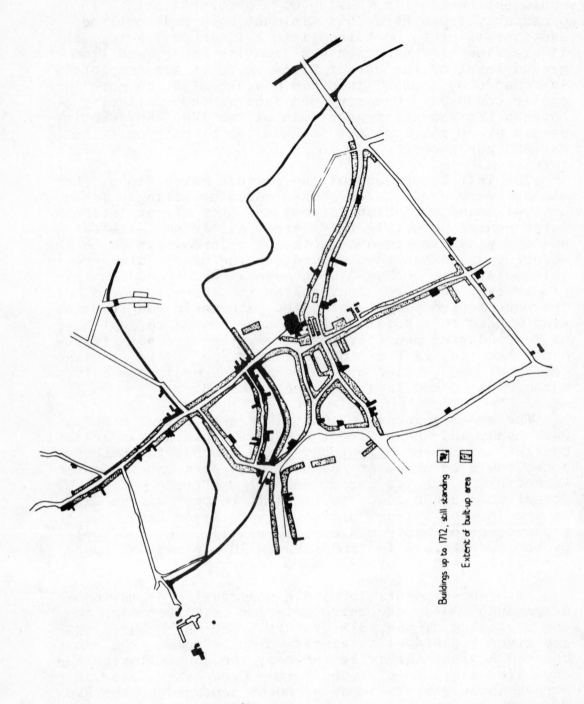

Fig. 6

Cirencester in the 17th C.

In terms of growth and town planning there is little change between the Kip plate and the map of 1793. The main changes affected individual buildings, the first being the Mansion itself which lost the form shown by Kip within four years of the publication of the view. It received a solid, rather uninspiring classical facade which has since been more or less hidden by later attempts to improve it. The rebuilding of the Abbey House after a fire c.1780, in so uninspired a form that no-one was able to give good reason why it should not be demolished in 1963, robbed the town of its only other major late 16th century building.

Few, if any, major buildings of classical influence or full classical style lie on freshly developed ground, they are almost all replacements for earlier buildings. Thus they lie in Dyer Street, Dollar Street, the Market Place, Thomas Street and the southern part of Gloucester Street, but less in the northern part of Gloucester Street, Cricklade Street, and the extremities of Dyer Street and Castle Street, all of which, by then, were perhaps the poorer parts of the town. One cul-de-sac which became extremely fashionable at this time was Cecily Hill which was eventually robbed of its path out of the town to Minchinhampton and Bisley by the formation of the Park and the building of the new Stroud Road. Here in the 18th century a full range of developing building styles occurred so that we can trace the change from the Cirencester style of Coxwell Street into the classical influence of the older part of 5 and the magnificent facades of 32 and 40-42. Gothic tracery in the brick bow addition to 3 and in part of a wing of 40 point to awareness of the Gothic revival, the use of Cecily Hill lintels is dated on 11-15, and in 19 we have either the first stirrings of Cotswold revival with mullions and drip-moulds in a classical facade, or else genuine survival of a very pleasing kind.

The 18th century is one of consolidation, replacement in new styles, and a good solid vernacular style in stone, rather than one of growth; to it we owe some of the finest buildings, and also some of the very simple buildings whose survival provides an architectural light and shade and a pleasing background to later developments.

References

1. All references to the original documents quoted for the time of the Dissolution of the Monasteries will be found in R. Reece, Trans. Bristol and Glos. Arch. Soc., 81, 1962, 198-202.
2. Prints in the Bingham Public Library, Cirencester.

THE GROWTH OF THE MODERN TOWN

All statements in this section, other than observations made during the survey, are due to the excellent documentation in Beecham, <u>A History of Cirencester</u> (Cirencester, 1886), to which page numbers refer.

Our survey of buildings stops in 1921 and the outline commentary on the town as a unit must stop there also. Though it may seem arbitrary not to follow the town through to the changes attendant on the ring-road currently under construction there are two good reasons for such omission. Firstly the development of the town since 1920 has been very different from that which has happened since the foundation of the Roman civitas capital for between c.AD 75 and 1920 nearly all growth, shrinkage, or change was the result of individual owners of land and buildings, or, at most, a consortium of individuals. In AD 75 we have to presume that Roman provincial authority acted on behalf of the natives and ordered the development of the town; there may even have been a show of democracy, and a trained planning adviser may have been seconded from the army to assist the ardo or council of the tribal area (civitas) in laying out its capital town. In the 20th century again planning authorities and councils rule and Cirencester no longer grows, but is developed (note the passive voice). Thus it is fair to insist that the growth of Cirencester ceased around 1920 when development took over. This leads to the second reason for not tracing change in the town beyond 1921: the development is in mid-course. In a few years' time with a completed ring-road and concomitant building schemes, the development of Cirencester from 1921 onwards will be in a resting stage and can be assessed and described.

In 1800 the town scarcely filled its presumed medieval limits and was virtually confined to the boundaries of the medieval borough in and beyond the northern half of the Roman walled area. The Chesterton tythe map of 1807 (see p.) shows no substantial buildings along Watermoor Road, and the Stepstairs Lane area seems empty but for barns. The growth of the town started in 1826 with the sale of Watermoor Common to provide funds for the clearance of Shoe Lane and Butter Row from the centre of the Market Place. Beecham, who is the main source for this section, comments that a "vent for the pent up population was afforded" (p.186). There is little support for his statement in the census figures which he quotes (p.195) and which are reproduced below, although it may be that the majority of 124 extra houses for 1831-1851 belong to the period shortly after 1830.

Buildings after 1712 and up to 1795, still standing

Buildings up to 1712, still standing

Fig. 7

Cirencester in the 18th C.

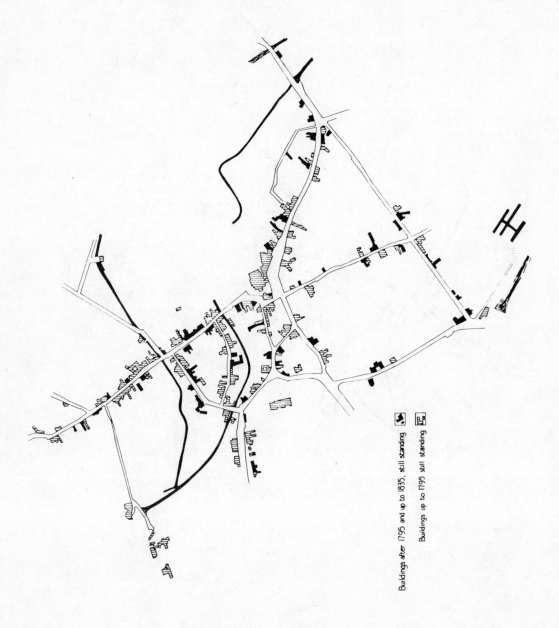

Buildings after 1795 and up to 1835, still standing

Buildings up to 1795 still standing

Fig. 8

Cirencester in the early 19th C.

Date	Inhabited Houses	Increase	Inhabitants	Increase
1801	837		4130	
1811	926	89	4540	410
1821	1006	80	4987	447
1831	1079	73	5420	433
1841	–	134	6014	594
1851	1213		6096	82
1861	1300	87	6334	238
1871	1455	155	7079	745
1881	1484	29	7739	660

The land marked as Watermoor Common on the 1807 map lies south of Siddington Road in the angle it makes with the Cricklade Road. No housing seems ever to have been built here so the 1826 expansion must have taken place around Stepstairs Lane and the parallel frontage of Watermoor Road, together with the south side of City Bank Road (now replaced by modern houses) and a row nearby on the east side of Watermoor Road. These houses are interesting in that they are fairly firmly dated examples of middle-class classical houses whose style was to be copied in the growth of Watermoor right into the 1880's.

In 1853 the growth started in earnest with the sale of the Pitacres Estate - presumably the land in the east angle formed by Somerford Road and Chesterton Lane - and The Nursery to the south of Lewis Lane. The Nursery is often referred to as Gregory's Nursery after the family who ran the business. Small remnants of Gregory's nursery remain, worked by their successors Messrs. Jefferies, beside Tower Street, at the end of City Bank Road, and on the south-west side of the Cricklade Road. Carpenters Lane formed the east boundary of the land, according to the map of 1837, and this line was continued by hedges and fences south-south-east to the end of City Bank Road. Remnants of this line could be seen in a row of apple trees beside the field of the former Grammar School in Victoria Road, in the alignment of that school's cricket pavilion, set against the row of apple trees, and in the irregular path which runs in front of the terrace City Bank View. A similar remnant accounts for the odd alignment of 2 and 4 Queen Street, built with their back walls against undeveloped Nursery property.

The first buildings on this land were probably those of Watermoor House. J.R. Mullings became articled as solicitor in Cirencester in 1820 and married a Miss Gregory in 1823; after working for a while away from the town he returned in the late 1820's and settled down. This presumably dates Watermoor House between about 1828 and 1835 when it appears on Wood's map, carved out of the Gregory acres. The Gregorys however did not own the land for Beecham records that Chester Street is named after T.W. Chester Master "to whose family the land belonged" (p.187).

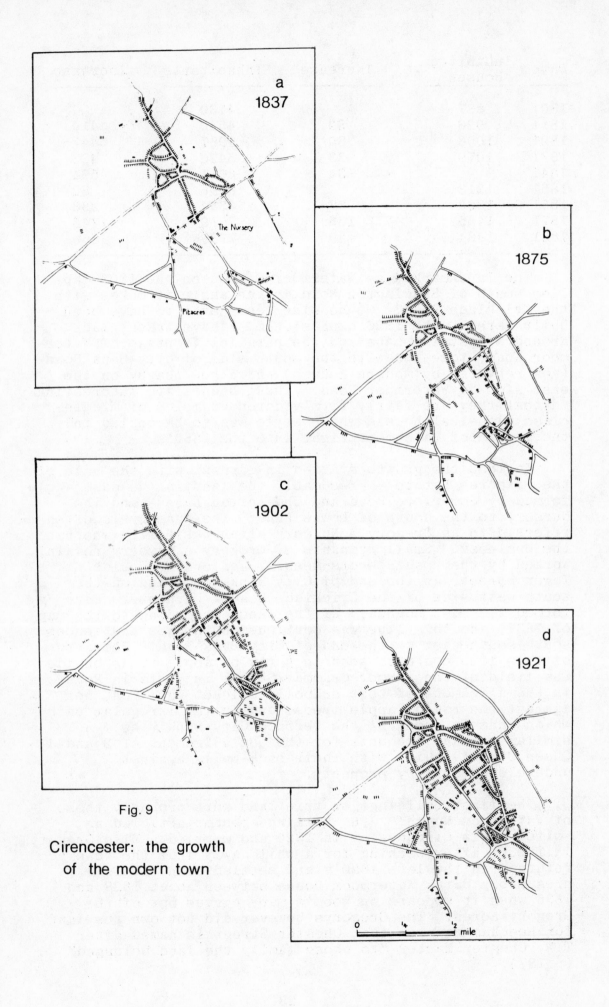

a
1837

The Nursery

Pitacres

b
1875

c
1902

Fig. 9

Cirencester: the growth
of the modern town

d
1921

0   ¼   ½ mile

From 1853 to about 1860 little happened, but the next decade produced record results in house building and it seems likely that most of these houses belong to Chester Street, Tower Street, and the west side of Victoria Road. In 1870 the east side of Victoria Road was "mapped out in single house plots, but a lull had set in in building, and no lots were sold until 1878" (p.187). Brick appears, as noted in more detail below (see p. 58) around 1875 in Tower Street, and in less exalted form, in Queen Street in 1880 and 1885.

Mount Street and Somerford Road - presumably "the land between (Pitacres) and the Querns" (p.186) was sold c.1861 and the superior plots on the west side of Somerford Road in about 1873. All areas have some houses on by 1875 though the decade 1871-1881 only appears to provide 29 extra inhabited houses. By this time the two major styles seem to be houses either in rough stone or in brick. This is presumably a difference in price, and presumably in class. The styles develop together on the east side of Victoria Road where houses in rough stone are typically semidetached and often of three stories with front and tradesman's door, and large front drawing rooms projecting in angular bays from the facade. Servant's basements are not common and seem to belong to the 1870's-1880's rather than the years around 1900. In contrast, the brick houses of the 1880's and 1890's are more towards the Watermoor end of the town; they form simple terraces more often of two stories with much flatter facades and few attempts at detail save for a seemingly obligatory bay window. The brick styles connect up building projects in Victoria Road, Watermoor Road, a terrace in Beeches Road, and then from 1890 onwards in Ashcroft where brick and rough stone develop side by side. The final phase of terrace building started about 1906 when Purley Road was laid out. After an experiment in off-white brick the plan changed to red-brick with the upper floor rendered with pebble dash. This succession suggests that terraces in plain red brick were no longer acceptable so that some effort had to be made to enhance their appearance. Building continued in Purley Road and Purley Avenue, in Chesterton Lane, Mount Street, Cotswold Avenue, Sperringate and Siddington Road after the end-date of our survey but the four square terrace set nearly on the road was then no longer in fashion. Large developments have taken place at Chesterton and the Beeches, but there whole estates have been laid out as planned units and red brick has been banished from sight by smooth rendered surfaces.

One aspect of growth which Cirencester has almost missed is the Victorian professional man's villa. The large houses in Somerford Road, Elmgrove, Southleigh, Magpies and others belong to this class, as do Leaholme and 1 and 3 The Avenue. A few houses in Victoria Road may be added, but even here there are rows of substantial houses and blocks of two rather than the gracious residences of North Oxford or some of the wealthy London suburbs. Not until the development of Berkeley Road, an extreme outpost of the Somerford Road complex, and the Whiteway in the 1930's, 40's and 50's do there seem to be areas of detached houses. Perhaps it was not until recently that the town was large enough for desirable villas to perch on the edge without fear of the encirclement which happened in Victoria Road, Ashcroft, Beeches Road, the Avenue and the Whiteway. This has ensured a considerable social mixture, at least in the older part of the town, which has continued to the present day.

The other end of the scale, the smallest cottages, are much more difficult to discuss because they have been cleared away in extremely determined fashion in the last thirty years. Opening off Gloucester Street, Dyer Street, Cricklade Street, Dollar Street, Thomas Street and Coxwell Street were Yards, Courts, Alleys, Rows and Places, all consisting of a long narrow open space with small cottages along one side. On the map of 1875 the extreme regularity of these cottages - small rectangles in a row - strongly suggest that each block was built as a unit. Unfortunately both 28-38 Black Jack Street, and Sheppards Place, Gloucester Street look the same on a map, as does the 14th century Arlington Row at Bibury, Glos. While it is possible to be sure that these demolished rows lay in date between Arlington Row and Black Jack Street, it is impossible to locate them any more exactly in time at the present. Of the two town examples left 28-38 Black Jack Street is a row of about 1840 while the entrance to Sheppards Place is dated 1694 and some of the houses are almost certainly earlier. It is unsafe to argue from existing examples simply because they do still exist and have not been removed; they are presumably in better condition and may therefore be more modern, or have been better built. One sign which suggests that some of these rows may have belonged to the early 19th century is the existence on the 1837 map of a small collection of such houses on Stepstairs Lane and School Lane which are not on the Chesterton Tything map of 1807. The same is true for Prices Row in Watermoor Road. Stepstairs Lane, Midland Road, and School Lane were removed only a few years ago so thoroughly that even the lines of the roads can no longer be traced; they have been replaced by a somewhat austere development known locally as "the Concentration Camp". No adequate records were kept, and I doubt whether many photographs exist. In this way a piece of the town vital to the understanding of its development has been thoroughly excised so that the question of Places and Rows must be left unanswered.

A final point is the form into which the town had grown by 1921. Apart from the growth of Chesterton it is fascinating to see how the town grew slowly back into the limits set for it in the 70's of the first century AD. Apart from Gloucester Street, Somerford Road and the Gasworks and Railway south of Watermoor, the limit of the built up area in 321 and in 1921 is given roughly by a circuit starting at the junction of Grove Lane and London Road (the Roman Verulamium Gate) going by Grove Lane, Spitalgate Lane, Thomas Street, Park Street, Park Lane, Sheep Street, Querns Road, School Lane, City Bank Road, the City Bank and Beeches Road, back to the point of departure. This line is now being emphasised by the construction of a ring road which will encapsulate the early nucleus, hopefully returning it primarily to a residential area rather than a junction of busy holiday routes.

PAST, PRESENT AND FUTURE

There is little pressure on those who undertake
surveys, excavations, or historical projects to make them
relevant to the business of living in the modern world.
Relevance is even seen to conflict with scholarship, to
be an undesirable constraint, or, in its worst form a
publicity stunt or a futile attempt to justify socially
an unnecessary and unproductive past-time. A well
conceived excavation or historical project will have in
it the seeds of its own relevance. The excavation should
attempt to make sense of a community, or a part of a
community, and not waste its time trying to convince a
public which is only marginally interested that three
postholes of a Roman building rescued from destruction
represent a treasury of knowledge. The historical project
must of its very nature proceed from the relics of a
community to recreate, comment on, and explain that community, or a part of it. Both pursuits should make the
workers in each field well fitted to bring their studies
up to the present and thus to comment on the life of the
current communities. It is even arguable that it is only
possible to interpret any part of the past through a
knowledge of, and immersion in, the present so that the
two are not only linked, but cannot be separated. These
comments are therefore offered, as an integral part of the
study, not as an apologetic footnote.

Two main areas of disagreement are at once obvious;
what should come down, and what should go up. The earlier
a building the stronger the case, presumably for keeping
it standing. A glance at fig. 6 will show how few of the
buildings which Kip saw at the beginning of the 18th
century are still visible. The situation is a little
better if we consider the buildings represented on the
map of 1793 which still stand, but it seems obvious to
say that these buildings form so small a part of the
present town that we cannot afford to lose one without
exceptional reasons being given. Yet one 18th century and
early 19th century building has been demolished while this
study was being done, one of the few half timbered cottages
surviving was under attack two years ago in 1972, and an
excellent 18th century stone frontage was saved by public
enquiry in 1973. In all these cases developers claimed
that their motives were of the purest, that they would
never move an important building, but that these examples
were not great of their kind, and had come to the end of
their useful life. It would be kindness, they argued to
put down these faithful friends rather than let them
linger on in unsatisfactory condition. A new building is
always described as intending to fit harmoniously in with
the surrounding varied townscape, so that any change might
almost be for the better.

Opposed to the persuasive voices of the demon developers are some who would prefer no change to happen to the

architecture of the town. Neither side seems to take into
account the place of buildings in the life of a community.
The buildings of a town form the material back-cloth
against which every single activity of the community takes
place. It is a street of houses through which we go to
school, to work, to shop, or to while time away; it is a
building in which we are born, grow up, get married, grow
old, and die. However small the effect may be these
surroundings do have some effect on us, and a community
which does not care about its surroundings does not care
about its own life; as a consequence it deserves from
its surroundings help proportional to the attention which
the surroundings receive.

    When it is proposed therefore that a building be remov-
ed and replaced it is worth each person stopping to think
whether this change will improve or detract from his
surroundings. He knows the building there at present, he
knows the associations it holds for him, he can decide, if
he stops on the way to work for a moment to think about it,
whether he positively likes the look of the building, or
feels no affection for it whatsoever. He can look at the
examples already in the town of recent building and can
make up his mind whether these would improve this site or
not. If he can see no likely improvement the case is
settled; the old building must remain. If he can see
probable improvement a discussion must take place with
people who see the opposite, and if the community will
find its surroundings improved by change, change there
must be.

    It may be noted that economics have not entered into
the argument. This is not woolly idealism, but simply
the recognition of a great advantage which many towns with
old buildings share. There are many people about who wish
to own and to live in old buildings, buildings with
associations, buildings which look attractive, or simply
buildings which their neighbours do not live in. Whatever
their motives there is available a large amount of private
money for the restoration of older buildings to form
desirable residences. The answer to any business, firm
or developer, who pleads that it is uneconomic for him to
restore, convert, or exactly rebuild a building, is to
suggest that he should sell it to someone who will.
Unfortunately such suggestions are unlikely to be well
received, for the sale of premises bought for business
purposes at prices relevant to living accommodation is
likely to produce a financial loss. The answer for the
recalcitrant owner is to let a few more slates slide from
the roof, encourage death-watch beetle in the timbers,
and the building will soon fall down, if it cannot be
knocked down. The rubble can then be cleared away and
a site is available for development.

    It is possible that an answer to this nonsensical
state of affairs may approach the statute book in the
reasonably near future. All that is necessary is the

power for a statutory body to require the owner of a
building to repair it, or sell it. A building whose
demolition has been averted will then have to be returned
to good order within a reasonable length of time, or sold,
in that same time. Faced with such a threat a developer
will either find that the building was not such an unusable
shell as he thought, and start on renovation in his own
interest, or he will decide that there is little of profit
in the building for him and sell it. But the financier to
whom he wishes to sell it will be aware of the law, and
will fight shy of such a responsibility when he can build
a brand new headquarters elsewhere, and the original
developer will have to sell the house for a reasonable
sum to a family willing to spend time and money making a
home of it.

This brings us on to a subsidiary danger, one perhaps
nearer to archaeological detail. To what extent may a
building be changed? After many years of rather thought-
less demolition we are entering a phase of well-meaning
restoration. With a few extra windows, a floor raised
a few feet, a new doorway, though the old one looks a
nice feature tastefully blocked with plants in the walls,
The Old Button Factory, in a quiet part of town, may hope
for a new lease of life.

In one way this has never happened before. Buildings
have very often changed purposes, doors have been blocked,
windows have been opened up, and whole stories have been
added or subtracted, but the purpose up to the very
recent past has been to produce a functional new building
of the appropriate specifications. This seems obvious,
honest, and therefore satisfactory. The present mode of
restoration is dishonest in that a house is a space for
living in, and a building cannot be an honestly made house
if living is either artificially constrained by the
surroundings, or if a compromise has been made between
honest living requirements, and historical detail. If, in
a wall containing two small early windows, three new larger
windows are inserted and the two older ones retained in
obviously unsatisfactory and unusable positions, it would
probably have been better to take out the early windows,
donate them to the museum, and design something with the
aim of living in it. The occupant of a ravished house
derives little benefit from dishonest antiquarian detail,
the spectator sees on the outside a designed mess. The
alternative to starting again is, of course, to live
voluntarily within the original walls. The rooms will be
low, small and dark, but there are many people whose life-
style this will suit. Not to allow people to live in such
surroundings is official idiocy at its worst.

A project in which all the buildings in a manageably
small town have been scrutinised briefly therefore leads
us to these conclusions. There are probably no buildings
more than 150 years old (pre 1830) which the town can afford
to lose without changing itself and losing something in the

process. Some styles of building of the middle 19th century and later are at present so well represented that some examples could be spared, other styles are rare, and so need protection even if no one feels greatly for them at present. Which brings us to the second great question, what should go up?

In Verey's volume on the Cotswolds in the Buildings of England series he reaches the year 1919 with the comment "It would be nice to be able to stop this introduction here, and on further consideration there seems to be no valid reason for not doing so..." (p.63). We have stopped our survey only two years later, with the third edition of the Ordnance Survey in 1921, and this has happened partly through the same feelings that Verey expressed. Faced with rows of modern houses, some with intricate detail, some with no detail at all there seemed no point in recording and analysing a style with no purpose, no direction, and no originality. Yet some attempt has to be made to assess modern architecture, or at least see some of its possibilities. In a small town, well off the architectural mainstream it is probably better to try to examine the question historicially; what has happened before?

It is debatable as to whether there has ever been a Cirencester or Cotswold, or even West Country style of architecture. The earliest wooden framed buildings in the town are similar in general design, though not perhaps in detail of construction, to wooden framed buildings elsewhere. The earliest stone buildings are ecclesiastical and any suggestion that the perpendicular style was one peculiar to the Cotswolds would arouse extreme disagreement in East Anglia and many other parts of England. As soon as classical details were introduced any semblance of local style fled in favour of copies of great buildings designed with mediterranean models in mind. The classical influence continued in default of other inspiration for a considerable time in Cirencester until it was challenged by revivalism, in which Tudor was far more obvious than Gothic. Verey again sums it up in his presidential address to the Bristol and Gloucestershire Society (Trans., Vol. 92 for 1973, p.5) "it was agreed by most people that Gothic was the proper mode for churches, Elizabethan for houses, and Italian for municipal buildings". Running absolutely true to form at this time Cirencester shows Holy Trinity Church, Watermoor in the Gothic style, the Corn Hall in the Italian style, and Oakley Cottage in the Elizabethan style.

There is one style that has been missed out of this melancholy list of Cotswold plagiarism, and that is the style in which most of the superior houses of the later 17th century were built. With its combination of medieval survivals and simple common sense this combination of a good stone facade with details only at the windows and the doors, and one or two gables breaking the facade, with stone tiles set on a roof of moderately steep pitch this

fashion is at once homely, satisfying, and stately. The
windows usually have stone mullions and transomes, or
mullions alone, and the individual drip moulds or long
continuous drip moulds are the only details which project
from the surface of the facade except perhaps for the
decorated head to a moulded doorcase. Even here the
details are collected together from other styles which
grew well outside the Cotswold area; the mullions and
mullions and transomes have come from the stone tracery
of the latest medieval gothic windows, and the mouldings
of the doorcases show often the flat tudor arch and
renaissance detail in the head which presumably is of
Italian extraction. The spacing of the windows with
their size carefully regulated according to their height
in the building, the gables with no overhang, but a
single timber lying on the stone and visible immediately
under the tiles, and the floor joists and the roof beams
appearing flush with the exterior stonework having been
carried through the wall all combine to produce an
impression of design with nothing but essential details.
And this design, or craftsmanship delights many people.
Why does a typical building erected in Cirencester, or
any other small town in the last thirty years not equally
delight people? What ought the modern architect to do in
order to achieve this good taste once again? To hope to
answer these questions is ridiculous yet to discuss them
is necessary, and discussion must start somewhere. It
seems obvious that one good place for such discussion is
at the end of a historical survey.

The modern building is not built of stone except in a
few cases. In Cirencester the architect has to design in
reconstituted stone, and no doubt similar requirements
exist in other places which are trying to avoid gross mistakes
in modern development. As yet it seems obvious that no
architect has learnt how to use reconstituted stone. It
is at present being used as a substitute for either concrete
blocks or real stone and the buildings which it faces therefore look either like concrete barracks or pastiche copies
of the late 17th century style. The first requirement is
presumably that architects shall explore the possibilities
of this new material in which they are being forced to
build so that they may design buildings for the material
rather than using it as a substitute.

But this well meaning directive to build only in stone
or reconstituted stone may itself be partly responsible for
the low standard of design which is now obvious. It is
doubtful if such a constraint will be acceptable to an
architect who actually wants to say something through his
buildings rather than wanting to design an unexceptionable
shell in which any activity can conveniently be carried on.
It may be that the right course is to choose either an
architect who has proved himself elsewhere and let him
loose on a design in the town, whatever the materials or
design, or else to ask for several general essays for one

single commission, then to select the best. This suggests
competition, and it is interesting that none of the major
developments in the town have been thought important
enough to launch an open competition to attract new and
varied ideas to the new buildings of the changing townscape.

Attempting a further statement of the ways in which
most modern buildings offend, or more often, fail to please,
we probably need to consider the roof-line. The first fully
horizontal roofline came in with the classical cornice and
parapet, it is therefore probably of little use to single
out the modern flat roof as an item of disfavour, for the
same criticism would apply to many classical and sub-
classical buildings which are generally found to be pleasing.
It is worth noting that the flat roof is always associated
with a foreign or intrusive style, so that the use of gables
might assist a new building to blend better with pre-existing
buildings. Another feature which seems unsatisfactory in
many modern designs is the total lack of detail, moulding
or emphasis at the doors and windows. Again, this point
is of little use for this is true of larger houses such as
5 Dyer Street, surely a major asset, and on smaller houses
of the whole of style II from the 18th century.

Irregularity however seems to be a problem. Style I
buildings and especially the late 17th century kept a very
careful balance of features, and in most instances actually
employed perfect symmetry of features. As designs moved
toward the classical it was perfectly possible to have the
door to one side of the facade with perhaps three bays of
windows on one side, and four or five on the other. Where
perfect symmetry was not used, but an attempt was made at
balance then the asymmetry was obvious and calculated. Two
aspects of irregularity would seem difficult to accept in
some modern buildings; the alignment, or non-alignment
with the street frontage, and an irregular angle or lop-
sidedness of a gable. There is obviously nothing intrin-
sically wrong in irregularity, and no doubt modern examples are carefully calculated, but their effect is often
that of a deliberate mistake. Few, if any, earlier
buildings in the town are set at an angle to the frontage;
in one or two recent buildings where this has been done
it is uncertain if it is intentional or whether this has
resulted from alignment of a rectangular building with
some other feature such as a property boundary. Similar-
ly, some modern tilted gables give an impression only of
imbalance. In neither case has the irregularity been
thought out carefully enough with regard to the surrounding buildings which are inevitably regular, and having
decided to use an irregularity the architect has not been
strong enough to make a point with it, so that it has
misfired.

A last point contradicts what has just been said, for
one of the most unpleasant aspects of modern buildings
when part of a row of earlier buildings is the blatant
regularity of window heights instead of a pleasant grada-
tion from the ground floor upwards. This is a purely

subjective statement with no firm basis but prejudice,
and it suggests something which is to be firmly rejected,
that some features of architecture are immutable. There
is no reason that we can see, save custom, and what is
seen most often, why buildings should have windows which
get smaller the higher they are, yet it appears as a
jarring mistake when a new building forces the feature of
uniform windows into a row of older houses all following
the older fashion. Perhaps we have here a point that has
already been mentioned under the previous heading of
irregularity. If a new building is departing from the
style of its neighbours it needs to be in dialogue with
them. It cannot be self contained and successful. A
facade on a slight angle with delicately asymmetrical
gables will be shouted down by a neighbouring row of
19th century facades which are overpoweringly sure of
themselves and refuse any innovations by their side.
Delicacy or tentative design is useless, what is needed
is a full bodied argument from a brash newcomer of sure
design, strong clean line, which shouts out one main
point in opposition to its pompous elders.

If the new building is not hemmed in by older neighbours but in a surrounding of its own then there is no
excuse for clients, architects, planning committees, or
the public at large if the design is not exciting,
controversial, confident, and therefore a contribution
to the town.

In the past the town has seen roughly one astonishing
building in each century. The Abbey was built at a time
when the new gothic style was appearing from France, and
although it had some firm Romanesque decoration its later
details must have used the newer style. The building of
the parish church, and additions to that and the Abbey
take us on into the 15th century. In the sixteenth
century the parish church porch, or Town Hall appeared
in fully developed perpendicular with oriel windows and
good fan tracery. The 17th century saw the development
of the Cirencester style, and then somewhere in the mid
18th century, a reactionary element produced the
magnificent facade of 51 Coxwell Street, and this was
challenged by the utterly intrusive brilliance of
Lloyd's Bank. The 19th century intruded an Italianate
facade into the staid Market Place, a building with no
local elements at all. We are due for our 20th century
inspiration, but it can never arrive if the town is
timid and correct.

THE SURVEY

a) Aim

The survey set out to examine every building in
Cirencester, to give it a date within known limits, and to
assign it to a style in which it would be grouped with
other similar buildings. A subsidiary aim was the study
of the development of the town.

b) Definitions and Limitations

To the native the definition of Cirencester is
obvious. In spelling it out for the less fortunate we
have tried to examine every building within the recent
Urban District, or modern town, excepting those farms on
the periphery which are still functioning as farms, or
were doing so until recently, e.g. Chesterton Farm, Bowling
Green Farm, etc. Buildings not shown on the map of 1921
have been excluded. They are listed as G in the index,
without further comment, if they occur in streets with a
majority of older buildings. Where there are no pre 1921
buildings in a street, the street is not mentioned.

The term building has been limited mainly to the
facade, which has been studied at first hand, except where
vegetation made this impossible, and the ground plan,
which has been studied from maps. In many cases we have
certainly dated a building too late, but before the date
can be revised there must be physical evidence on which
to proceed. Outbuildings have, in general, been excluded;
apart from the difficulties which would have been
encountered in classifying summer-houses, dog kennels,
gardening sheds and garages, the time involved in gaining
access to each building would have been prohibitive.

c) Sources

Five maps of the complete town of Cirencester at a
suitably large scale are known to us. In the last years
of the 18th century an enterprising surveyor Richard Hall
made a map of the town of which he drew several copies;
on different copies he outlined the properties of various
landowners, added a suitable ascription, and the larger
estates thus received "individual" treatment. One copy -
dated 1793 - dedicated to Henry, Earl Bathurst, is in the
Bingham Library, Cirencester, a second copy in the
Gloucestershire Record Office (D 2525) shows "the
property of T.B. Howell Esq."; it is from a photocopy of
this map kindly supplied by the Record Office that we
have worked. The map gives street names, identifies
inns, marks gardens and open fields and gives most
property boundaries. On details of buildings it is
brilliantly exact down to the details of bow windows and
uneven facades. Though it is a great pity that there
seems to be no earlier complete map it would be impossible
to be better served for the end of the 18th century.

The "Plan of Cirencester 1835" by John Wood, Surveyor
- also supplied by the County Record Office (D 6746 P 48)
as a photocopy - is far less accurate than its predecessor.
Buildings are sometimes conventionally drawn, details are
omitted, and sometimes buildings are completely wrong.
It is possible to make this criticism with safety because
there are instances where the maps of 1793 and 1875 agree,
but 1835 differs. One great bonus in 1835 is the naming
of all property according to its owner. This has not been
used much in the present study though it has provided much
information for use in future work. Wood gives the population of Cirencester in 1831 as 4,998. Beecham (p.195)
presumably using official census figures, quotes 5,420, a
discrepancy of nearly ten per cent. It is impossible to
compare Beecham's number of houses, 1,079 for 1831, with
the map for only property boundaries, not boundaries
between living units, are shown.

The first edition of the Ordnance Survey for Cirencester
was surveyed just one hundred years ago in 1875 by Capt. L.
J.G. Ferrier, RE, and levelled by Lieut. W. Wynne, R.E.
It was published, apparently in the same year, at the scale
of 1:500. The 25 inch to the mile, or 1:2500, edition of
1875 was apparently surveyed and levelled in 1873-74.
The largest scale (c.6 feet to one mile) gives an invaluable insight into the details of Cirencester a century
ago; we hope to follow this in much greater detail in a
future study. New editions of the 1:2500 map appeared in
1902, 1921 and 1970. The second and third editions are
useful for charting the growth of the town in the decades
around 1900, while the fourth edition gives much needed
help, but occasionally spreads confusion, on the matter of
street numbers for buildings. Photocopies of all but the
fourth edition, 1:2500, were kindly supplied by the
British Library, Reprographic Section, and Mr. Mark Webber
helped by finding the relevant sheets and editions.

Chief among the other maps available is that in Beecham
opposite p.250, which gives a plan of the town in 1886.
Unfortunately the scale of 10 inches to the mile only
allows of accurate interpretation in the well spaced
developments of Watermoor; it is probably more danger
than help in the more densely packed older part of the
town. But this interim view of Watermoor, which allows
two phases, Ei 1875-1886 and Eii 1886-1902, between the
first and second editions of the 1:2500 Ordnance Survey
is of the greatest value.

One of the chief defects of the 1793 and 1835 maps is
that they show little of the town to the south of the
Lewis Lane - Querns Lane line. This is partly remedied
by the "Map of the Borough of Cirencester, 1837" drawn
by J. Dewhurst at a scale of five inches to the mile.
This map, supplied as a photocopy by the County Record
Office (D 2525) gives all the outlying buildings erected
by 1837 and can therefore be taken as a complement to,

and a check on, Wood's map of 1835. It gives the Borough
and the Tything boundaries, though in built up areas
these are difficult to follow. The "Plan of the Tything
of Chesterton" drawn in 1808 by Hall and Son for Henry,
Earl Bathurst, a copy of which was used by the Estate to
note details of land conveyanced to the Great Western
Railway Company on 30th December 1846, is in the County
Record Office (D 2525), and this gives the vital division
between the tythings of Chesterton and Sperringate.
Other maps of parts of the town do exist but are of very
limited use. Kip's plan has already been mentioned in
detail.

Moving from plans to written sources the quality drops
sharply. The history of Cirencester has always been
cumulative so that each writer has repeated what his
predecessor has had to say and has added to it from his
own knowledge. While not a perfect historical method
this has preserved much of value, especially when it is
remembered that each writer will be most useful and most
accurate when reporting his own times; few people around
1800 will have checked on Rudder's antiquarian statements
but disagreement will have been strong on any mis-state-
ment of contemporary points. This is not the place to
attempt a Cirencester bibliography, but we may note in
passing that the cumulative comments of Atkyns (The
Ancient and Present State of Gloucestershire, 1712)
Rudder (A New History of Gloucestershire, 1779; A History
of Cirencester 1800) and W.K. Beecham (A History of
Cirencester, 1848) have little to say on individual
buildings or useful dates. Rudder's thoughts on old
buildings have already been quoted. This leaves the three
more recent historians of Cirencester, K.J. Beecham (History
of Cirencester, 1886), the Rev. E.A. Fuller (several
detailed papers in Transactions of the Bristol and
Gloucestershire Archaeological Society, Vols I-XXVIII)
and Welbore St. Clair Baddeley (A History of Cirencester,
1924). Fuller's papers are excellent, detailed, historical
studies of specific topics - the parish church, the school,
the Abbey - and he can therefore be absolved from his
failure to help us with information on secular buildings
in general. The contrast between the two remaining writers
could not be greater; Beecham is superb, Baddeley is
disastrous.

For Baddeley the history of Cirencester ends c.1700,
of the Bathurst family c.1800, and all that we are given
of the 19th century is an afterword by W. Scotford Harmer
which, though very valuable for its reminiscences, gives
very few firm dates for buildings. Beecham, in contrast,
is a nearly perfect source for the Victorian buildings of
Cirencester. Having trained as an architect he was
extremely conscientious in noting the date at which all
major buildings were erected, and he charted the development of the Nursery (Watermoor) and Ashcroft Estates
meticulously. For him the modern barracks (p.236, 1856)

37

are as important as the ancient castle, the Corn Hall
deserves as much description (p.229) as Alfred's Hall in
the Park, and the details of the Gasworks are given at
greater length than those of St. John's Hospital. Only
on one subject is he silent, and that by design (p.312)
the people of Cirencester.

The most obvious direct written source for buildings
apart from the 1851-71 census returns, which we hope to
work on shortly, are their deeds, or in a few cases,
inscriptions on the facades. We have noted all the
inscriptions we have seen, but we have not consulted any
current deeds. Many boxes of Cirencester deeds deposited
by defunct solicitor's offices and estates are housed in
the County Record Office. In a few cases the properties
to which the deeds refer are identified, but for the
majority the only details are, for example, "a shop and
messuage in Cricklade Street". It seems a reasonable
summary to say that most deeds which have found their way
into the record office have lost their modern counterpart
so that any hope of using them for quick and certain
dating is vain. A long thorough project would be needed
to make the right use of this valuable untapped source.
If any house-holders in Cirencester are willing to look
at deeds still in their own possession and let us know
the results in terms of dates, inhabitants and functions,
whether they prove us right or wrong, we will be very
grateful and will undertake to publish an amended list in
due course.

The aim of this study was material; to describe, and
to begin to analyse the buildings and the physical surroundings which exist in a small town today. To a very small
extent we have taken advantage of oral sources and have
received valuable help, information, and ideas from Mrs
Barker, Mrs Elphick, Mrs Young, Mr. J. Clappen, Mr.
Clayfield, Mr. H. Legg, Mr. & Mrs R.M. Reece, and Mr. D.J.
Viner. A survey of buildings of Cirencester was needed
because the primary source, the buildings, are constantly
being removed. The primary source on the community within
these buildings, the memory of the community itself, is
being eroded at an even faster rate by the natural course
of illness and death, and in a few years memories of the
proper Cirencester, before 1918 when the outside world
intruded, will be gone. If we have succeeded in laying
the barest outline of systematic knowledge of the skeleton
of a society, its buildings, then we hope to go on to tap
as many oral sources as we can to endow these buildings
with remembered life, and to improve the outline in the
process.

d) Methods

The first stage of the study was a detailed tour of
all buildings in the town. A list was made of the street
numbers to be expected from the 1970 Ordnance Survey
1:2500 and a tabular description of each building was made,

street by street, in a ledger. In all cases the date
was guessed, and this purely subjective guess not only
proved on several occasions to be remarkably accurate,
but also saved us from many slips due to the too rigid
application of a system of classification at a later
stage. The second stage was the digestion of the
information gathered and an attempt to sort the buildings
into consistent and informative groups. A completely
objective sorting and grouping would have given fascinating results but this obviously needs electronic help and
was far beyond our time and our resources. Within the
date brackets given by the maps (1712, 1793, 1835, etc.)
we did use a simple matrix of features and this laid the
basis of the final classification which cut across the
date brackets and relied largely on assessment of style.
This grouping is partly subjective, in that certain
features had to be treated at the expense of other
features which were considered less important for grouping,
and partly objective, in that once the vital features had
been selected the grouping became mechanised, i.e. all
buildings with features X, Y and Z were put in style II.

The division into styles in most cases required a
second visit to check the features which were now
considered important; this provided a useful correcting
process. Divisions within styles took a considerable
time, and though all attempts have been made to use only
simple and obvious groupings, there remain some unsatisfactory groups and attributions. The style lists were
finally checked with the record cards, and the index made
out, in which all buildings of the town before 1921 were
included. This again formed a cross-check which revealed
gaps and mistakes and these were rectified. An estimate
of accuracy is virtually impossible, mainly because there
are few tests of what in this field, is right and what is
wrong. Perhaps we can hope that no more than one in
twenty (5 per cent) of our entries may be shown to be
factually inaccurate or stylistically inept; if this is
so it means that this first attempt at a complete survey
of the buildings of Cirencester has provided a reasonably
firm foundation for future research.

e)   Summary of Conclusions

The traditional methods of writing up a piece of
scientific work, especially an experiment requires that
Aim, Method and Observations should be followed by a
Conclusion. This may be no bad thing for it forces any
writer who accepts the discipline into an estimate of
error - a feature lamentably lacking in archaeological
and historical writing - and a summary of what the work
has achieved. We have yet to find many archaeological
reports in which the writers honestly state dissatisfaction
with their aims, their methods or their results, and we
have certainly never seen a report in which either a
historian or an archaeologist admits that the results
obtained are far below those normally required by the

expenditure of the given amount of money, time, effort
and expertise. Our balance sheet, in these terms, has
been set out in the preface, and we feel that it is
satisfactory. What, therefore, do we claim as results?

In the commentary we have suggested a framework for
understanding the growth of Cirencester from a simple
river ford, a Roman fort, a Civitas capital, the capital
of the province of Britannia Prima, a post-Roman city
state, a Saxon royal residence, a small medieval town
controlled by one of the greater mitred Abbeys, a
flourishing wool town and finally a quiet market town,
centre of a large country area. If, in ten years time,
the introductory chapters do not need complete revision
it will mean not that we were correct in our suggestions
but that no further thinking on the subject has been done.
These first chapters use as few uncertain facts as
possible, as many reasonably certain facts as can be
gathered, and as little unsupported imagination as can
be attained; they deserve critical attention and
constructive comments.

In the survey every building erected before 1922 and
standing in August 1974 has been put into a stylistic
group by virtue of its architectural or structural detail,
or lack of it, and has been given a date to within half a
century or less. From this work we have been able to make
comments on the use of brick which is rare in facades
before about 1875. If this development is to be laid at the
door of improving communications it is hardly due to the
Thames and Severn Canal (1790's) or the Great Western
Railway (1841); it is interesting that the "Midland and
South Western Junction" railway travelling from the clays
of Hampshire, reached Swindon in 1875 and Watermoor in
1883. The first two brick terraces (p. 58) are of 1880
and 1885. After this beginning brick flourished briefly
before being part shrouded in stucco (c.1906-14) and
latterly banished from sight.

The use of types of building stone may probably be
understood more easily now that most buildings have been
given a rough date. Simple dressed Cotswold freestone
occurs at all periods though apart from the clerical and
charitable buildings of the town the earliest houses are
timber framed. Many of these timber buildings have a
stone plinth and stone foundations, but the stone built
houses with gables, using timbers mainly horizontally,
which are thought of as typical Cirencester houses,
seem to be a development of the 17th century. Ashlar
facing, in which large blocks of smooth stone are laid
without intervening courses of mortar, first appears on
Lloyds Bank, perhaps soon after 1740, but does not come
into common use until the 1790's. Even after that it is
by no means universal. It is interesting to speculate on
the re-organisation needed in the quarries when the
demand for ashlar facing grew. The working of stone
quarries is a fascinating area of research which seems so

far virtually untouched except for the recent excavation
of a group of Saxon quarries at Ewen, three miles from
Cirencester.

The building of Watermoor Church (1847-50) in what
Beecham describes as "rock faced masonry" of forest marble
seems to be the first use of very rough stone facing apart
from the natural limestone formations used in the entrance
gateway to Cirencester House and occasionally elsewhere
for keystones. Many buildings follow in this rusticated
style but seldom, if ever, in the forest marble used at
Watermoor.

Turning from methods to styles the survey helps to
separate out the buildings with classical features into
those which precede the full classical style - mainly 1795-
1835 - and those buildings in which classical features
have lived on. This allows mention of one of the points
at which our guess dates were most obviously inaccurate,
for the proto classical buildings with heavy dressed
window surrounds were seen as late classical decline
rather than early classical influence. In the same way,
rough dating has allowed us to suggest thoughts on the
survival and revival of early features such as drip moulds
and mullions and transomes, the minor Romanesque revival,
and the absence of any full 20th century "Town Hall
Georgian".

But perhaps the main value of the study lies in what
may be done in the future with such details of the
development of planning and buildings of a small town,
fortunate in its supply of superb building stone, but
many years away from the mainstream of architectural
style as it has developed in England since the Reformation.

MEDIEVAL BUILDINGS

Without doubt the three earliest buildings in the town are the Saxon Arch, St. John's Hospital and the Parish Church (all originally c.1180). Since these are isolated examples of early architecture which have been thoroughly dealt with in other works it is not necessary to describe them here.

The earliest secular building to survive is Weavers Hall of Thomas Street, built by Sir William Nottingham, Attorney General to Edward IV "for the benefit of four poor men" and endowed at his death in 1483 (Beecham, pp 223/4). It has a plinth made up of very large stone blocks, has several very small deep set windows and one crude window with a heavy mullion and transome. It seems possible that four single light windows placed near to each other, gradually coalesced to form four lights within a single frame, as in this particular window, and eventually evolved into the more delicate Tudor mullioned and transomed window such as those of Monmouth House in Thomas Street. Both Monmouth House and 26 Thomas Street probably date from the early 16th century.

Style I

Style I consists of buildings with stone mullions, stone mullions and transomes, either individual or continuous drip moulds, and coved eaves as their characteristic features. The earliest buildings in this style have individual drip moulds, and mullioned windows. Mullioned windows can be sub-divided into three groups of concave moulding, chamfered moulding or ovolo moulding. The earliest buildings are recognised by their concave mouldings, which may be a contemporary secular reflection of the 15th and 16th century windows in the Parish Church. Thus buildings in Phase I(b) are probably late 16th or early 17th century.

It is not possible to say definitely whether ovolo or chamfered mullions are used first because there is only a two year difference in date between the two earliest dated buildings employing this ornamentation. However the latest form of moulding to be used on stone window frames in Cirencester buildings is flat beaded moulding of style IVa. It is more obvious that chamfered moulding could have evolved into flat beaded moulding than that ovolo moulding should have done; this would suggest that chamfered moulding was the later style. Furthermore there is a tendency for buildings of this style to become less ornamented the later they are, which would again make the plainer chamfered moulding the latest style. It is therefore reasonable to suggest that buildings with ovolo mullions were built after 1640, and chamfered mullions after 1660.

This tendency of later buildings to be stylistically

less detailed is also observable in the development of drip moulds. The individual drip moulds which are found in conjunction with stone mullions gradually evolve into continuous drip moulds. 25 Coxwell Street perhaps represents a transition stage between the two since it has a continuous drip mould which is shaped over the heads of windows. Both types of drip mould are found on some buildings, but in all these cases the individual drip mould is found on the ground floor windows and the continuous drip mould relegated to upper storeys. No individual drip moulds appear on buildings later than 1700 until they are re-adopted by the "antiquarian revivalist" architects of the 19th century.

During the 17th century, the proportions of buildings were changing as ceiling levels were rising and rooms becoming taller. This affected the proportions of windows used in a building, for if the Cirencester builder had continued to use mullioned windows in taller buildings the windows would have resembled prison grilles. However he responded by rotating the long axis of the window frame from the horizontal to the vertical. Extra support for the now heightened mullion was gained by the addition of a horizontal cross bar - the transome. Mullioned windows were still used in conjunction with mullioned and transom-ed windows but only on upper stories and in gables, where the height of the storey made it appropriate.

105 Gloucester Street, dated 1695, is the only dated building with stone mullions and transomes but buildings of this phase probably go back to 1670.

Coved eaves are a feature of Style I which appear only on buildings which have no gables on the facade. This is also connected with the development of buildings of taller proportions, since there is only one mullioned building with coved eaves. This building is the Unitarian church and it is also exceptional in being the only building with mullioned windows which are taller than they are wide. As this is an ecclesiastical building it is not surprising that it deviates from the secular pattern.

I(a) Buildings having individual drip moulds and single mullions

Concave Moulding   Coxwell Street: 1 - also has a moulded stone doorcase dated RM 1658
Park Street: 11

Watermoor Road: 2, Chesterton Manor has two concave and two ovolo mullioned windows.

Ovolo Moulding   Coxwell Street: 25 - also has a moulded stone doorcase dated 1674
Cecily Hill: 27
Castle Street: 43

Gosditch Street: Unitarian Church – also has
coved eaves and a keystone arch doorcase dated
1672.

Chamfered   Gloucester Street: 7 – also has a moulded
Moulding   stone doorcase dated 1694.
                Gloucester Street: 2-6 – (these may be a
                later reconstruction of earlier buildings)

I(b) Buildings having continuous drip moulds and single
     mullions.

Concave
Moulding   Gloucester Street: 40

                Coxwell Street: 2 – also has a moulded stone
Ovolo   doorcase dated ERE 1676
Moulding   Coxwell Street: 5
                Park Street: 9

Chamfered   Gloucester Street: 19
Moulding   Gooseacre Lane: 11 and 15

I(c) Buildings having continuous drip moulds and stone
     mullions and transomes.

                Park Street: The Old Grammar School – also
                has mullioned windows
                Park Street: 1 and 3 – also concave mullioned
                windows in the gable, possibly reused, and a
                continuous drip mould which is shaped over the
Ovolo   rounded heads of the ground floor windows.
Moulding   Coxwell Street: 53
                Dyer Street: 2 and 4 – also has coved eaves
                Lewis Lane: 16
                Dyer Street: 39
                Coxwell Street: 3
                Beeches Road: The Golden Farm
                Castle Street: 15, The Black Horse

                Cricklade Street: 44
                Cricklade Street: The Wheatsheaf
                Castle Street: 63
Chamfered   Park Street: 2 and 4 – also has coved eaves
Moulding   Sheep Street: 29 and 31 – also has coved
                eaves
                Gloucester Street: 57, Barton Court –
                Gloucester Street: 105 – also has moulded
                stone doorcase dated BBI 1679

I(d) Buildings with coved eaves.

                Thomas Street: 6 – also has a continuous drip
                mould
                Market Place: 28 and 30
                Cecily Hill: 2 – also has continuous drip mould
                Castle Street: 22-26
                Cricklade Street: 72 and 74
                Dollar Street: 1 and 3

44

I(e) Buildings with continuous drip moulds as their only
      stylistic feature.

            Gloucester Street: 28, 51 and 53
            Coxwell Street: 14-20
            Dollar Street: 4 and 14
            Dyer Street: 9 and 11
            Lewis Lane: 14 (probably replaced with stucco
            band course)

Style II

     Style II consists of timber framed buildings, defined
as buildings in which the weight of the facade rests on
the timber frame. Other buildings with timber frames,
whose weight rests on a stone facade are not included in
this category but are classified by the features of the
stone facade. All the buildings in this category have
visible upright timber supports, and all have a jetty.
Probably 16th/17th century.

            Dyer Street: 12, The Bear
            Market Place: 41, The Fleece - also has a
            stone plinth
            Dollar Street: 6 and 8
            Gloucester Street: 33 and 35 - also has a
            plinth of very large stones
            Gloucester Street: 96
            Castle Street: 19 and 47
            Gosditch Street: 17 and 19
            Gloucester Street: ? 141

Style III

     Style III consists of buildings with no other stylistic
detail than a single block lintel above the door and window
jambs. The earliest phase in this style consists of
buildings with timber lintels some of which have leaded
casement windows. It is probable that all the timber
lintelled buildings had leaded casements originally but
some have been replaced with modern windows. Timber
lintels appear on buildings dated pre 1715 and as late as
1875, when they are falling out of use with the wider use
of monolithic stone lintels. Buildings in category (c)
continue the tradition of this style of featureless
buildings, but with the substitution of stone for timber
as a building material, and date from pre 1835 to 1921.

III(a) Buildings having timber lintels and leaded case-
        ments as their only stylistic feature.

            Market Place: 35
            Castle Street: 17 and 45
            Coxwell Street: 27-37
            Spitalgate Lane: 1 and 27

45

Barton Farm and farm buildings
Gloucester Street: 88-94 and 169-177
City Bank Road: 14 and 16
Beeches Road: The New Mills
Tetbury Road: The Toll House
London Road: 6-10, Grove Cottages
Thomas Street: 27-37
Querns Lane: 23
Querns Hill: 43-47

III(b) Buildings having leaded casements and modern
        lintels, probably replacing timber lintels.

Gloucester Street: 26, 95-97 and 185
Castle Street: 3
Park Street: 15
Barton Lane: 10 and 12
Lewis Lane: 32-38
Dugdale Road: 14-16

III(c) Buildings having timber lintels as their only
        stylistic feature.

Cricklade Street: 48, 50, 60 and 89
Gloucester Street: 60
Castle Street: 45 and 53
Black Jack Street: 12
Somerford Road: 16
Black Jack Street: The Crown Garages
Gooseacre Lane: 1-3
Coxwell Street: 32 and 36
Park Street: 19
Cecily Hill: 3
Sheep Street: 35
Waterloo: 14 and 16
Thomas Street: 47
Gloucester Street: 56 and 58, 62-66, 98 and
100, 102 and 104, 114-118, and 120
Spitalgate Lane: 2
Gloucester Street: The Nelson extension
Gooseacre Lane: 2-4, The Nelson Hall
Querns Lane: 25 and 54
Watermoor Road: Queens Head Garages

III(d) Buildings having monolithic stone lintels as their
        only stylistic feature.

Cricklade Street: 39 and 41
Dollar Street: 20
Park Street: 17
Dyer Street: 37 and 41
Gloucester Street: 74, 91 and 93
Black Jack Street: 44
Cricklade Street: 62
Watermoor Road: 28, 38-48, 54-58, 64-76, 95
and 135-143
Victoria Road: 86-96

        Tower Street: 12-16 and Jefferies Nursery
        Avenue: 15 and 17, 22, 24 and 34(a)
        Chester Street: 60 and 62
        Church Street: 2 and 4, 11-15, 25-27, 36-40,30
        City Bank Road: 1, 3 and 10
        Prospect Place: 2-20 and 32-38
        Ashcroft Road: 6
        Bridge Road: The Gasworks Office
        Somerford Road: Highfield Cottage and Magpies
        Chesterton Lane: 56-60 and 66-72
        Stroud Road: Ammonite Cottage, dated 1888
        Siddington Road: The Horse and Drill
        Watermoor Road: The Queens Head
        Spitalgate Lane: 3-9
        Queen Street: 2 and 4
        London Road: The Apple Loft

Style IV

     This group of buildings is rather more arbitrary than
most of the other styles for it comprises mainly buildings
in transition from the last stages of Style I, Cirencester-
Cotswold to Style V, Cirencester-Neo Classic. The point at
which a building gains enough classical details to achieve
a transitional or full Classic status, is bound to be
subjective, and this is the main cause of arbitraryness
in the group. Renaissance and classical details appeared
commonly in Style I - mainly associated with doorways and
doorcases; windows of Style I stayed firmly non-classical.
In group IV(a) there are classical keystones in the window
lintels, or window surrounds, and the last phase of
mullions and transomes. The end product of the mullion
and transome tradition can be seen in the White Lion
(c.1726), Gloucester Street, with keystones, and in the
magnificent facade of 51 Coxwell Street (? c.1740) whose
sombre elegance is so severe that it achieves the classic
ideal in simplicity and proportion while relying on
Cirencester-Cotswold details to the exclusion of all
specifically classical ornament. In the Little Bull,
72 Dyer Street, the mullion and transome tradition seems to
run into the classical ashlar style complete with band
course, and the date of 1791 on the earliest deeds in the
Gloucestershire Records Office (DC E 51) seems quite
acceptable.

     Group IV(b) is a collection of buildings, still in
dressed stone, rather than ashlar, but often very well
cut blocks, which have projecting rectangular window
surrounds with keystones. They fall into two divisions
one with round headed windows (mid 18th century ?) the
other with square heads. Moving towards the end of the
century we have a small group of stone buildings whose
main decorative feature is this same rectangular projecting surround to doors and windows (IV(c)) which is
presumably near the end of the 18th century since its
features carry on to full classical facades such as the
Wharfingers House (Style V).

                              47

The last group of buildings (IV(d)) all have Cecily
Hill lintels as their main, or only feature. This lintel,
made up almost of voussoirs laid to form a completely
horizontal arch (Plate III) is first dated on 11-15
Cecily Hill (1777), and seems to be used indiscriminately
on great and small stone buildings at the beginning of
the classical style. It is soon dropped from the
fashionable repertoir as the classical style develops and
is left for the humbler buildings of two storey tenements
such as Wood's Square, 59-67 Gloucester Street or Brady's
Cheese Warehouse, 3 Querns Lane. The style dies in the
1840's as brick is imported in small quantities for
lintels and other detail.

IV(a)   Stone mullions and transomes on stone buildings.

	Coxwell Street: 51	
	Black Jack Street: 7	
	Gloucester Street: 3 and 5	
	Dyer Street: 72	
Flat	Coxwell Street: 47 and 49	
beaded	Cricklade Street: 64-66	
Moulding	Cecily Hill: 9	Keystones
	Gloucester Street: 8	

IV(b)   Projecting window surrounds with keystones on
        stone buildings.

Cricklade Street: 10 and 12	
Market Place: 9-17	
Dollar Street: 30	Round headed
Black Jack Street: 2(a)	
Silver Street: 4 and 6	
Castle Street: 23	
Siddington Road: 6 and 8, Goldschmidt Arms	

IV(c)   Stone buildings with heavy dressed window surrounds.

Thomas Street: 8
Gloucester Street: 10
Gloucester Street: 16-22
Watermoor Road: Chesterton Manor
Thomas Street: Friends Meeting House

IV(d)   Stone buildings with Cecily Hill lintels as their
        main or only decorative feature.

Cecily Hill: 11-15
Barton Lane: 6-8 and 28
Beeches Road: 1-5 and 9-19
Silver Street: 7-9
Park Street: 5-7
Castle Street: 69-71
Querns Lane: 3 and 5-17
Sheep Street: 23
Spitalgate Lane: 11-21
Thomas Street: 2 and 25 Little Mead

Coxwell Street: 12a
Gloucester Street: 30, 37-49, 59-67, 83-85,
87-89, 111-117, 143 and 106-112
Cricklade Street: 76-82 and 91
Watermoor Road: Coles Mill
Lewis Lane: 85

Style V   Cirencester Neo-Classical

This category consists of buildings with classical
details which appear on the maps of 1793 and 1835, in
other words built before 1835; an arbitrary division
which is justified in Style VI. The buildings have been
further subdivided into stone, stucco and ashlar faced
buildings. As the buildings of Style IV are faced in
rubble or well cut blocks and the first phase of Style VI
consists of ashlar faced buildings it might be assumed
that stone precedes ashlar with stucco forming a
transitional phase between the two.

The two points of departure for the neo-classic style
in Cirencester are provided by Lloyd's Bank in Castle
Street and Cirencester House. Built in the first two
decades of the 18th century these represent two extremes
of a style, Lloyd's Bank being a building of intricate
detail while Cirencester House is plain and unadorned.
4 to 28 Cecily Hill, the Tontine Buildings of 1802
reflect the sparseness of detail in Cirencester House,
while 40 and 42 Cecily Hill has a wide range of detail,
following the exhuberance of Lloyd's Bank. A feature
connecting both of these buildings, and 32 Cecily Hill
with Style IV is the Cecily Hill lintel. Chesterton
House and Watermoor Hospital are later buildings with
stone facades, moving towards the severity and lack of
detail common in Style V. Buildings with stucco suggest
a desire for facades with a smooth surface, in the
tradition of Lloyd's Bank.

7 Cecily Hill has an ashlar addition to the original
stucco faced building so that the combination of stucco and
ashlar first seen in Lloyd's Bank is repeated but with a
gap of half a century between the two parts. 60 Dyer
Street, Gloucester House, is a stucco faced building at
the height of the Adam style c.1780. 45 Coxwell Street
is another stucco faced building with two entrances; these
are a somewhat pedestrian Roman doric porch, the other an
attractive doorcase with Etruscan overtones. The Wharfingers
House, Querns Hill uses the heavy dressed window surrounds
with keystones of Style IV in a full classical composition,
features consistent with its date late in the eighteenth
century. 20 Thomas Street extends similar details into a
fine stucco facade using stone for Gibbs surrounds to doors
and windows.

Earlier ashlar buildings, for example 32 Dollar Street

and 5 Dyer Street, have very plain facades with no window
mouldings; simple porticos add to their imposing
austerity. Although this appears to upset the sequence
proposed there seems to be no doubt that these two buildings appear on the map of 1793 whereas 18 and 20 Thomas
Street are built later and are similar to their ashlar
contemporaries 22 Thomas Street, 29 Park Street and 3
Dyer Street. Of these three buildings, 29 Park Street is
rusticated on the ground floor and has window heads
similar to those of the Gibbs surrounds of 20 Thomas
Street; the other two are almost exact copies in ashlar
of 22 Thomas Street but without the elaborate window and
door surrounds.

Ashlar faced buildings towards the end of the period,
such as Watermoor House c.1830, appear to lose control
over their classical details so that they no longer form a
harmonious whole.

V(a)   Buildings with classical features pre 1835 with a
       stone facade.

         Dyer Street: 7 and 17
         Market Place: 19, 23 and 37
         Gosditch Street: 3-5
         Thomas Street: 49 and 51
         Park Street: 6 and 8, 12 and 14 and Dunstall
         House
         Cecily Hill: 5, 4-28, 32, 40 and 42
         Black Jack Street: 6
         Castle Street: 18
         Querns Lane: 1, 19 and 35-39
         Park Lane: Cirencester House
         Chesterton Lane: Chesterton House
         Watermoor Road: 145 and 147
         Watermoor Hospital
         Sheep Street: 25
         West Market Place: 11
         Silver Street: 2
         Coxwell Street: 39-43

V(b)   Buildings with classical features pre 1835 with a
       stucco facade.

         Dyer Street: 3, 5, 57, 60 and 84-86
         Market Place: 25, 29-33, 38-40 and 43
         West Market Place: 3(a)
         Gosditch Street: 7, 9, 9(a) and 11
         Dollar Street: 10, 12 and 32
         Gloucester Street: 107
         Thomas Street: 20 and 22
         Coxwell Street: 6 and 45
         Park Street: 29
         Cecily Hill: 7
         Cricklade Street: 5 and 7
         Querns Hill: The Wharfingers House
         London Road: 5-7
         Black Jack Street: 8

V(c)   Buildings with classical features pre 1835 with an
       ashlar facade.

> Castle Street: 14, Lloyd's Bank
> Dyer Street: 33, 53 and 55
> West Market Place: 2 and 4, 5 and 7
> Market Place: 1, 3, 5 and 7
> Dollar Street: 7 and 9, 43-45
> Thomas Street: 12-16 and 18
> Gloucester Street: 12, 14 and 29
> London Road: 15
> Castle Street: 31 and 33
> Watermoor Road: Watermoor House

Style VI

The classical style of building took roughly a century
to take root in Cirencester (c.1700-1800), blossomed briefly in a reasonably pure form (c.1800-1835) and decayed
slowly (c.1835-1939). Any division between classical and
sub-classical is bound to be subjective; an attempt has
been made towards objectivity by taking as a dividing
line the map of 1835. Thus buildings on the map, built
before 1835 are taken to be sound classical, and the later
buildings are listed mainly as a falling away from classical design. Anomalies are present and usually commented on,
but the dividing line proves reasonably acceptable in
practice. The buildings have been divided into four main
groups according to the finish of the facade: VI(a) contains buildings faced in ashlar blocks, VI(b), buildings
faced with dressed stone, VI(c) buildings faced with
stucco, and VI(d) buildings faced with rusticated stone.
The majority of ashlar facades seem to belong to the middle
19th century, stucco to the second half of the century,
smooth and rusticated stone to the end of the 19th century
and beginning of the 20th century.

Amongst the ashlar facades after 1835 there are a few
pleasant surprises. The garden (south-east) front of
the Beeches House, Beeches Road, presents a simple, if
slightly gloomy, classical aspect, whereas in 21-25 West
Market Place, Chesterton Terrace (16-26) Watermoor Road
and the Gasworks Cottage, Bridge Road, the simplicity of
detail and satisfying proportions give a clean and
welcoming atmosphere. In the same vein is the small block
44-50 Victoria Road, soon after 1853, a remarkably
attractive and homely sub-classical building. Highfield,
Somerford Road (inscribed 1868) and 44-46 Lewis Lane are
the only examples of coursed chamfered ashlar. The later
large villas of Somerford Road, Elm Grove, East Cranhams
and Rooks Nest (c.1870-75) use many of the other classical
motifs sometimes in odd combination; the Romanesque porch
of Elm Grove being worthy of special mention. The large
facade of 12-22 Market Place belongs to the end of the 19th
century (1886-1902), and the former Independent Methodist

Chapel - now the Memorial Hospital Annexe in Sheep Street was revised from classical to sub-classical by V.A. Lawson as a War Memorial in 1919.

With the move either forward in time to the end of the 19th century, or down the social scale, it is extremely difficult to wax eloquent over the general run of buildings which are uninspiring and uninspired. The Henry Tanner Chapel, 23 Park Street is simple and pleasant, Leaholme, 2 Avenue has at least some interesting details and 27 Sheep Street, a reconstruction of a Georgian House has some atmosphere.

Victorian sub-classical stucco is seldom pleasant, and sub-classical buildings with rusticated stone seem mainly out of sympathy with Cirencester styles. The best buildings in this group are perhaps 18 and 22 Somerford Road (1861-1875) and The Shrubbery, 97 Victoria Road, with its bay windows and pleasant doorcase.

Perhaps this grudging admiration of a few buildings of this type and dismissal of the majority is short sighted. This style represents the majority of mid Victorian building in Cirencester; at least it was restrained and in stone. This period produced many superb buildings in other towns but buildings of that high calibre are seldom seen in the work of the speculative builders who might have flooded the Nursery Estate with badly built, badly designed brick terraces, and gloomy middle class semi-detached villas. We ought to look again at the simple stone terraces such as the two storey blocks - 34-40 Chester Street - perhaps modelled on 42 without its re-used detail and be grateful for the friendliness of the stone, the light relief as blocks move up a few feet or back from the road, to give an impression of solid, gentle, if unremarkable domesticity.

VI(a)   Buildings with classical features after 1835 faced with ashlar.

              Beeches Road: The Beeches
              Watermoor Road: 16-26, 31-35 and 37-41
              Church Street: 17-23, 28
              Chester Street: 44, 46-48, 50-54 and 56-58
              Victoria Road: 16, 34-38, 35-37, 39, 40, 44-50,
              52-54, 95, and 98-100
              Cricklade Street: 14, 19-23
              Park Street: 10, 21 and 25
              Park Lane: 6
              Coxwell Street: Baptist Church and 8, Jehova's
              Witness
              Black Jack Street: 14, 16 and 18
              Castle Street: 35-37
              Thomas Street: 24, Friends Meeting House porch
              Market Place: 12-22 and 34-36
              West Market Place: 21-25
              Somerford Road: 12-14, 20, 30-36, Highfield,
              Elm Grove, Rooks Nest, East Cranhams

                Waterloo: 15
                Sheep Street: Hospital Annexe
                Ashcroft Road: 35-45
                Queen Street: 10, The Forresters
                Lewis Lane: 44-46
                Avenue: 8-12, 9
                Bridge Road: Gasworks Cottage
                Tetbury Road: Old Museum

VI(b)   Buildings with classical features after 1835 faced
        with dressed stone.

                Chester Street: 1-21, 2-14, 16-20, 22-28,
                25-75, 30-32, 34-40
                Queen Street: 1-5, 6, 7-15, 12-22, 17
                London Road: 9
                Watermoor Road: 27-29, Old Parsonage, 50-52,
                75, 83-87, 89-93
                Gloucester Street: 27, 70, 76-80, 103,
                145-7, 149-51, 187
                Victoria Road: 18-20, 22-24, 80-82, 102
                Chesterton Lane: Chesterton House Lodge
                Coxwell Street: 10a-b, 12
                Dollar Street: 51-53, 22 and 24, 28
                Castle Street: 20, 28, 32, 36
                Park Street: 23, 27
                Silver Street: 5
                Black Jack Street: 4, 24-26
                Lewis Lane: 35-37, 39-41, 83, 87
                Querns Lane: 21
                Cricklade Street: 32-36, Malt House
                Chester Crescent: 2-22
                Dyer Street: 10, 56-58, 60a, 62, 66 and 64
                Prospect Place: 1-3
                Sheep Street: 3-15, 27
                Avenue: 2, Leaholme, 14-20
                Somerford Road: 4-10, Southleigh
                Tower Street: 2-10, 18-22
                Mount Street: 1-3, 5-17
                Carpenters Lane: Furniture store
                Ashcroft Road: 56-58

VI(c)   Buildings with classical features after 1835 of
        stone (?) and stucco.

                Lewis Lane: 12
                Dollar Street: 11-17, 34
                Dyer Street: 6-8, 76-82, 43-45
                Market Place: 27

VI(d)   Buildings with classical features after 1835 faced
        with rusticated stone.

                Victoria Road: 4-6, 12, 56-60, 91, 97
                Dollar Street: 38
                Avenue: 19-21
                Ashcroft Road: 47-61

Ashcroft Gardens: 15
Tower Street: 24-26
Somerford Road: 18,22

Style VII

Although 2 and 4 Gloucester Street were included in
Style I, it was with misgivings since these buildings are
quite possibly reconstructed from pre-existing buildings,
and they serve to highlight the difficulty of distinguish-
ing between survival and revival buildings. 1 Grove Lane,
the Lodge to the Saxon Arch and 2 Dollar Street, also
illustrate this point being buildings using a declining
building style rather than being a conscious revival of
the style. 1 Grove Lane is rebuilt on the site of the
original lodge, with only small changes in plan to
distinguish it from the original, while 2 Dollar Street
could very easily be mistaken for an early building of
Style I if not for the fact that the river, over which it
is built, is shown as open on the 1835 map. 5 to 21
Watermoor Road, the Bowley Almshouses, dated by inscription
1826, are again a survival unlike the Lawson extension
opposite of 1924 which are revival. The use of a declining
building style set in contemporary surroundings is
illustrated by 19 and 21 to 25 Cecily Hill which have
stone mullions and individual drip moulds set regularly into
a tall ashlar facade with a parapet thus retaining the
proportions of a classical building but with features of
Style I.

After the abundance of classical and classical
influence buildings in Cirencester there seems to have been
a reaction against the regular facade in favour of a
building which would fit better into a rural background.
An active part in revival of Style I was given by the
Bathurst Estate which carried out a considerable amount of
restoration and rebuilding of their properties, and by
V.A. Lawson who designed both classical and revival
buildings in the town. Bathurst buildings are not only
recognisable by their inevitable and helpful inscriptions
bearing the Bathurst crest and the date of the building
but also by their stone mullioned windows and continuous
or individual drip moulds, to be seen in such buildings as
1 Cecily Hill, 38 and 40 Coxwell Street and 65 Thomas
Street. These same features are to be found in Lawsons
buildings, such as the Bowley Almshouses in Watermoor Road,
and Oakley Hall in Somerford Road, the latter being in
ashlar like the Bingham Library of 1904 in Dyer Street.
Ashlar is not a material used in Style I, but already the
Little Bull, Dyer Street, has proved its compatibility
with Cotswold features, as do the Querns, Tetbury Road,
dated 1825, and perhaps the first conscious revival
building in the town. The Querns has successfully used
steep gables, individual drip moulds and stone mullions,
on a large scale, without losing the impression of simplicity. These features are more usually found on cottages

54

such as 18 Dollar Street, the Kennels Lodge, Tetbury Road
and 9 to 21 Lewis Lane, the George Almshouses later re-
endowed by William Lennox, 5th Earl Bathurst; here stone
mullions and Tudor arch doorcases are more obviously in
keeping with the rural nature of the buildings. Simplicity
does not always go hand in hand with Cotswold features, as
15 Gosditch Street demonstrates, for this building, dated
1873, has a fantastic mixture of battlements and gargoyles
alongside stone mullions and transomes, individual drip
moulds and a tudor arch doorcase. Since a distinction has
been made between ashlar and stone faced buildings it would
be convenient at this point to state that these divisions
are again arbitrary. There seems to be no harm done by
dividing revival buildings into those of stone, ashlar or
rusticated so long as it is remembered that these are for
convenience only. The majority of survival and early
revival buildings are stone faced while ashlar contain a
cross section of buildings some of which are on the 1835
map while the latest do not appear until 1922. Rustication
is almost certainly used later than ashlar or stone since
the earlier rusticated buildings first appear on the 1875
map, and these seem to follow a style set by Sir Gilbert
Scott's Church at Watermoor built in 1850-1. Watermoor
Church is faced in rough cut stone while the Cemetery
Lodge and Chapels of Medland, and A.J.C. Scole's Church
and Presbytery of St. Peter break into full rustication;
all of these buildings have Victorian gothic windows.
The Temperance Hall, Gosditch Street also has Gothic
windows but resembles more closely the parish church
rather than Watermoor. The two schools of Lewis Lane,
1879, and Victoria Road, 1880, are also rusticated with
mullions and transomes, but by this stage revival architecture has lost its early simplicity and become mixed up
with elements of classical revival, such as pedimented
window heads and ballustrades. Unmixed classical revival
can be seen in 2 Market Place, the Midland Bank which has
a lead cupola, iron balustrades and a corbelled cornice,
and the Masonic Hall, the Avenue which has heavy dressed
window surrounds and a single Venetian window.

Besides Cotswold and Classical revival there are a
few isolated groups of buildings which have revived
features, such as 38 Cecily Hill which has herring bone
lintels, in imitation of the buildings either side and
opposite, as does 65 and 67 Castle Street, the Three
Compasses. Gothic revival is evident in the windows of
39 Market Place, 10 to 16 Park Street, 14 London Road,
Mill House, Watermoor Road, and the Town Station, Tetbury
Road. An attempt is also made to revive the exposed
timbers and overhanging upper storeys of timber framed
buildings in the form of half timbering, which is
successfully achieved in Lawsons buildings, 74 Dyer Street,
and 153 to 157 Gloucester Street and in the Memorial
Hospital, Sheep Street.

VII(a) Buildings having revived Style I features,
        faced in stone.

        Market Place: 39
        Gosditch Street: 1 and 15
        Dollar Street: 2, 3 and 18
        Gloucester Street: 32-86
        Barton Lane: 2 and 4
        Grove Lane: 1
        Thomas Street: 10
        Thomas Street: 65   Bathurst 1882
        Coxwell Street: 38 and 40
        Park Lane: 10-16
        Cecily Hill: 17, 19, 21-25, 29, 31 and 36
        Cecily Hill: 1 - Bathurst 1880
        Cecily Hill: 38 - dated 1909
        Black Jack Street: 10 - Bathurst 1909
        Castle Street: 5-7 and 65-57
        Castle Street: 40 - dated 1858
        Cricklade Street: 30 and 31
        Lewis Lane: 1-7 - Bathurst 1889
        Lewis Lane: 9-21, 18-30 and 2
        London Road: 11 and 14
        Tetbury Road: The Kennels - dated 1837
        Tetbury Road: The Kennels Lodge, Upper Querns
        Lodge and Oakley Cottage
        Chesterton Lane: Chesterton Farm Lodge
        Watermoor Road: 3, Mill House, Hopes Foundry,
        Watermoor School and School House, 4-14, 23-25
        and 77
        Watermoor Road: 5-21 - dated 1826
        Ashcroft Road: 48-54
        Dyer Street: 47-51 - Bathurst 1889

VII(b) Buildings having revived Style I features, faced
        in ashlar

        Tetbury Road: The Querns - dated 1825
        Beeches Road: The Beeches
        Gloucester Street: 54
        Tetbury Road: The Town Station
        Somerford Road: Oakley Hall
        Avenue: 4 and 6, 32 and 34
        Sheep Street: Marlborough Arms
        Dyer Street: 1 - dated 1904

VII(c) Buildings with revived Style I features with
        rustication.

        Watermoor Church
        Watermoor Road: 63-73
        Watermoor Road: The Parsonage
        Somerford Road: 2
        Cecily Hill: The Armoury
        Lewis Lane: The School - dated 1879
        Victoria Road: The Grammar School - dated 1880

Victoria Road: Stonewalls
Victoria Road: 8 and 10
St. Peters Road: 15, The Church and Presbytery
Castle Street: 2-12 - dated 1896/7
Avenue: 1-3
Chesterton Lane: The Cemetery Lodge and Chapels
Silver Street: 8-14
Black Jack Street: 9-17   Bathurst 1900
King Street: Bingham Hall - dated 1908
King Street: 2-28
Castle Street: 38 - dated 1910

VII(d)   Classical revival.

Avenue: Masonic Hall
Market Place: 2

VII(e)   Half timbered buildings.

Gloucester Street: 153-157 - dated 1906
Dyer Street: 74
Sheep Street: Memorial Hospital - dated 1873
Castle Street: 30
Dyer Street: 29-31

Style VIII

Buildings in this category have little stylistic
detail with which they can be categorised and so they have
been divided into stone faced buildings and rusticated
buildings.   A further division has been made between houses
and purpose built shops, public houses or engine sheds.
The majority of the stone faced buildings are later than
1835 but some earlier buildings have been included in this
category if they have no stylistic features.   All of the
rusticated buildings are later than 1835.   The only feature
which is held in common by a significant number of buildings
in this style is the angular bow window, but since there
appears to be no connection between the date of the building
and the style of the bow no distinction has been made
between wood, stone or bows with and without parapets.

VIII(a)   Houses with stone facades and no significant
features.

Avenue: 5 and 7
Prospect Place: 17
Gloucester Street: 25, 50 and 52 and 189-197
Querns Hill: 41, Querns Gables
Barton Lane: 40
Coxwell Street: 22-28
Lewis Lane: 52-56
London Road: 26 and 28
Somerford Road: 38 and 40

VIII(b)   Purpose built shops with stone facades and no
          significant features.

               Dyer Street: 35
               Gloucester Street: 48 and 122
               Dollar Street: 36
               Cricklade Street: 2, 4 and 40
               Castle Street: 9
               Watermoor Road: 97-103
               Black Jack Street: 2(b)
               London Road: 2-4

VIII(c)   Houses with rusticated facades and no significant
          features.

               Carpenters Lane: Argyll House
               Victoria Road: 2, 5-9, 26-32, 42, 41-49,
               95-81 and 99-101
               Church Street: 6-26
               St. Peters Road: 2-36, 3 and 5 and 9-15
               Mount Street: 2-6 and 20
               Chesterton Lane: 54 and 84-90

VIII(d)   Other rusticated buildings with no significant
          features.

               Watermoor Road: The Queens Head extension
               Victoria Road: The Talbot
               Bridge Road: The Engine Sheds

Style IX   Brick

Brick has been used as a building material in Cirencester at least since the 18th century, but until the middle
of the 19th century it was never allowed to appear on
facades. The side of the ashlar extension to 7 Cecily
Hill is good brick of c.1800 as is the "Gothick" bay
addition to the facade of 5 Cecily Hill. Perhaps the
earliest whole building to stand in clear unashamed brick
is the original Primitive Methodist Chapel in Lewis Lane,
built in 1851.

The breakthrough seems to come around 1875 for two
rows of brick buildings are caught in construction by the
map of that year. 159 Watermoor Road, stucco on brick
with stone details is on the map whereas 161-5 which are
virtually identical first appear on Beecham's map of 1886.
30 to 34 Tower Street, excellent large brick buildings
with stone decorative details and, surprisingly, stone
sides are on 1875, while 28, of exactly the same construction but set forward a little is first on 1886. The only
other brick buildings constructed for certain between
1875 and 1886 are 26-42 Queen Street (Beecham 1880) with
stone details and decorative eaves course and 19-37 Queen
Street (Beecham 1885), this time with a castellated red

brick eaves course. There are some other brick buildings
which appear on 1902 but not 1875 which cannot be more
closely dated because Beecham's map is not sufficiently
detailed.

Stucco (IX(a)) presumably on brick, appear in 8 and
10 the Market Place where in 8, however bleak the facade,
the Victorian architect deserves credit for a good try
at 18th century windows with architraves and an attempt
at a Gibbs surround; perhaps he should have enhanced the
consoles under the sills - in Cirencester at least, a
very Victorian habit. Brick partly rendered, stuccoed,
or with pebble dash blossomed in Purley Road, Siddington
Road and Mount Street, from about 1906, and flourished
well after our end date of 1922.

Yellow brick (IX(b)) is commendably rare. It appears
perhaps about 1870 at 2 Black Jack Street, perhaps 1880
at 20 Cricklade Street, with a burst in 1906 in the first
houses to be built in Purley Road.

Facades containing only brick with little or no
contrasting detail (IX(c)) are extremely rare, about the
only good examples being 83 to 89 Victoria Road dated by
inscription to 1906. By tradition the builder went bank-
rupt and the gardens to the rear were appropriated to
build 77 to 81, smaller, later, more modest houses, yet
with stone facades. This strongly suggests that this
unique block are due to speculation by a builder foreign
to the town who imported both style and materials, for
the excellent cast iron balconies and moulded bricks used
in door and window surrounds cannot be paralleled in the town.

Imposing brick buildings with stone details (IX(d))
are very few and seem to cluster around 1900. The large,
fully ornamented villas of the tradesmen are similar in
conception, while the Plume and Feathers (inscribed 1901)
Watermoor Road, and Castle Buildings (inscribed 1899)
Castle Street have a style of their own.

More modest brick buildings with stone detail (IX(e))
proliferate after the first steps in Queen Street (1875-
80) and continue perhaps up to 1914. Yellow brick, as the
prominent detail material only (IX(f)) thrives after 1890
and may be a short lived fashion.

The only buildings to use the heavily fired blue
bricks for decoration (IX(g)) are the superb buildings of
the Gasworks and Midland Railway near Bridge Road running
from 1896 to the dated Engine Shed of 1915. This "Brick
Romanesque" may suffocate many a modern town by its
industrial overbearance, but set in derelict land with
bushes growing from the cornices the style presents a
nostalgic twinge which may have fallen to the ring road
by the time this study is in print.

IX(a) Stucco on brick: ranging from a complete covering
       of fine stucco to a one storey cover of pebble dash.

            Market Place: 4, 6, 8-10
            Watermoor Road: 159, 161-5, 105
            Church Street: 34
            Victoria Road: 84
            Castle Street: 1
            Somerford Road: Laundry
            Ashcroft Gardens: 24
            Quadrangle, Bridge Road, Siddington Road,
            Nursery Road
            Purley Road: 2-12, 14-32, 19-21, 23-29, 31-41,
            34-44, 43-49, 46-56
            Purley Avenue: 2-4
            Mount Street: 25-31, 33-39
            Tetbury Road: Lower Querns Lodge
            Gooseacre Lane: 7-9
            Querns Lane: 38, 44
            Cricklade Street: 67-71, 81, Brewers Arms, 33,
            11, 42
            Ashcroft Road: 42
            West Market Place: 15

IX(b) Yellow or off white brick.

            Black Jack Street: 2
            Cricklade Street: 20
            Purley Road: 1-9, 11-17

IX(c) Red brick with little or no contrasting detail.

            Lewis Lane: Primitive Methodist Church
            Church Street: 1(a)
            Lewis Lane: 50, 54-56
            Victoria Road: 83-89
            Spitalgate Lane: 29
            Cricklade Street: 38

IX(d) Red brick with intricate stone detail

            Tower Street: 28, 30-34
            Lewis Lane: 48
            St. Peters Road: 1
            Ashcroft Road: 19-21
            Watermoor Road: Plume and Feathers
            Castle Street: 25-27 Castle Buildings
            Chesterton Lane: 45

IX(e) Red brick with minor stone detail.

            Queen Street: 26-42, 19-37, 24
            Cricklade Street: 44, 68
            Black Jack Street: 40-42
            Chesterton Lane: 33-43
            Somerford Road: 49-51
            Prospect Place: 7-15, 22-30, 5

                    Church Street: 5-9
                    Nursery Cottages: 2-16
                    Watermoor Road: 80-98, 102-116
                    Victoria Road: 69-73, 103-109, 111-125, 17
                    Ashcroft Road: 14-20, 22-26, 28-38, 40
                    Ashcroft Gardens, 1-11
                    City Bank Road: 27-43
                    Mount Street: 19-23
                    Castle Street: 51
                    London Road: 12, 20-22

IX(f)   Red brick with prominent yellow brick detail

                    Ashcroft Gardens: 2-22
                    Ashcroft Road: 1-9, Ashcroft Hall, Methodist
                    Church, Gloster Dairy, 11-17, 27-33
                    Watermoor Road: 109-113, 115-119
                    Avenue: 26-30
                    Chester Crescent: 24
                    City Bank Road: 5-27
                    Beeches Road: 21-27
                    Victoria Road: 19-21, 51-67

IX(g)   Red brick with blue brick detail.

                    Bridge Road: Engine Sheds 1886-1902 and
                    dated 1915, Gasworks on railway siding

Style X Miscellaneous

     The final style collects together a small number of
buildings which do not fit happily into any other style.
The number was greater, but the less remarkable buildings
have been forced into other styles leaving only ten
special cases.

a)   10 Coxwell Street. It is saddening, and a warning,
that the earliest dated house in the town (inscription
1648) has a doorway, but no other feature besides to give
us information. The facade is a simple 19th century stucco
composition unexceptionable were it not for the fact that
it is the result of "modernisation" which has hidden, or
destroyed a building which could help us understand part
of our surroundings. This is not a survey of detail but
a survey of buildings; with regret we must therefore
consign this house to the relative obscurity of 19th
century stucco. It is probably too much to hope that no
other early buildings are now, or will shortly, follow this
one into an architectural limbo.

b)   From the remarks made in official quarters on the
subject of removal of "sub-standard" housing we must assume
that two rows of early 19th century cottages have a limited
expectation of life. 28-38 Black Jack Street and 17-23
Waterloo are small stone cottages, with brick arched lintels

a link between the stone cottages of the turn of the 18th
-19th century, and the Improved Dwellings erected from
c.1860 onwards. As means to the understanding of the
development of Cirencester they are essential and should
remain especially as they are the only remaining examples
of many similar rows which appear on the 1875 map leading
off from Cricklade Street and Gloucester Street; as
houses for say single old-age pensioners, not able to do
handymen-jobs or make their own improvements, these
cottages are less than ideal. Surely the answer - rather
than compulsory purchase, demolition and expensive rebuilding - is to ensure that as such cottages come empty
they are sold to owner occupiers, perhaps two at once,
who will undertake to bring them up to standard. At no
burden to local rates an important part of a community's
history can be saved and people can own houses of which
they can be proud.

c)   1 and 13 West Market Place (left hand portion of Crown
facade) and 20 Black Jack Street (Golden Cross) are
welcome examples of 19th century exuberance. The first two
examples use a mixture of styles in stone and brick,
mostly covered by stucco to enliven the designs. The
Golden Cross is basically a stone facade with considerable
use of brick detail. Built before 1875 this presumably
shows the attraction which red brick decoration held for
some local patrons and builders. While one would imagine
that the imposing classical facades of 28-34 Tower Street,
despite their brick, have always commanded the approval of
"those who know", The Golden Cross must surely have
endured a period of aesthetic disapproval, for the
uninhibited use of red brick is vulgar; we agree - it is
vulgar - enjoyably so.

d)   Cirencester was lucky in attracting the services of
Medland to design, according to Verey, the Corn Hall
(1862) and the Kings Head (1835-75) in the Market Place.
Might one also add River Court, 29 Beeches Road (1886-
1902), on account of the fascinating composition of varied
elements and the surprising plaster mouldings under the
window head? Considerable encouragement may be derived
from the Corn Hall for here is a large ornate Victorian
stone building with no Cotswold features except its stone,
which is yet the brilliant point around which the Market
Place turns. This is encouraging because it means that
a really good architect, given his head, can produce a
masterpiece which need have no obvious links with the
intended site, and that building, through its own
brilliance will be worth having. At the same time, a
brilliant architect will design a building which will
fit into its surroundings, but he will do this implicitly,
intuitively or artistically, and the pettifogging
"guide-lines" of an uninspired committee will only turn
him away from the commission.

e)   Lastly we come to 42 Chester Street, built between

1859 and 1875, probably nearer the latter date. It incorporates an excellent doorcase with fluted pilasters, a moulded door head set over a keystone on a fluted lintel, and the windows have shouldered and fitted architraves. There seems no doubt that all the detail is genuine, yet every piece of old stone works fits perfectly on to the house and was almost certainly incorporated at the original build. Whoever built the house had a superb feeling for earlier detail. But all the nearby houses have identical dimensions without the detail. Did the builder build the row according to the proportions of one old house he demolished, or did he re-use older detail on a new design with consummate skill?

Figure (10) is an attempt to show, in graphic form, the chronological development of the styles listed in the catalogue, with the approximate dating provided by the maps on the vertical scale, and the styles and substyles on the horizontal axis. Therefore the graph shows in which periods a specific style is to be found, e.g. Style I(a) is only to be found on buildings pre 1712, whereas Style III(d) is found on buildings early enough to be shown on the 1793 map and late enough to be shown on the 1921 map; as it is therefore of little chronological significance it is put with Style VIII at the end. An arrow indicates that there are no existing buildings with, for example, Style IV(b) features built in the period 1795 to 1835. However, since Style IV(b) continues into the period 1835 to 1875 it is probable that there were buildings of the period 1795 to 1835 with these features, but which have since been demolished.

It is plain from the diagram that no style after IV(c) is to be found on buildings pre 1712 and with few exceptions no style before VI(a) appears on buildings later than 1835.

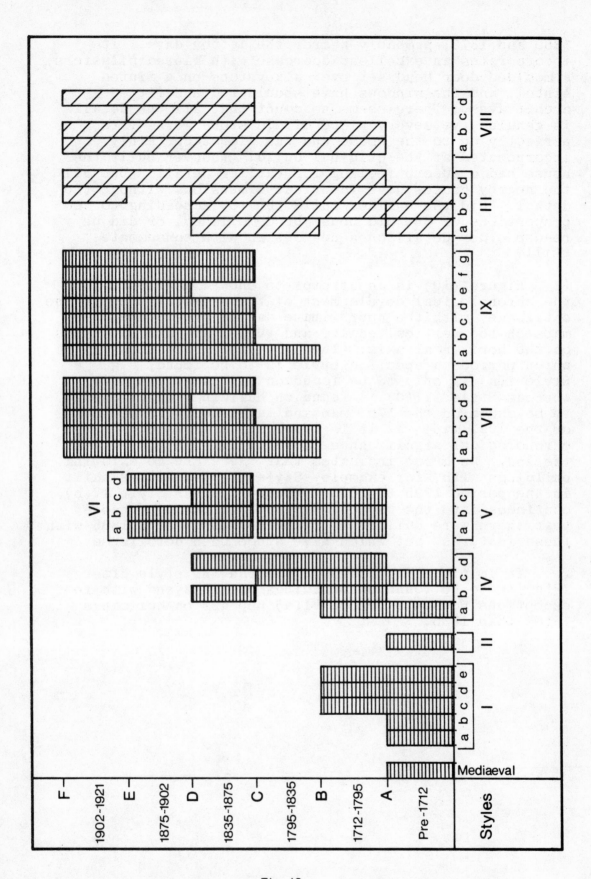

Fig. 10

Cirencester: Diagram of building features

INDEX OF BUILDINGS

Streets (see fig. 11) are listed in alphabetical order omitting "The" (Avenue, Market Place, Waterloo), and in each street buildings are given in numerical order with the even numbers in the left hand column and odd numbers on the right. Where buildings could have the same entry they are run together - e.g. Ashcroft Gardens 2-22 are all of the same style and date. Each entry gives the map on which it is reasonably certain that the building first appears by a capital letter:-

A   probably appears on the Kip print
B   map of 1793
C   map of 1835
D   first edition Ordnance Survey 1875 (1:2500)
Dii known from references to be late in D, e.g. 1855-1875
Ei Beecham's map of 1886
Eii second edition Ordnance Survey 1902 (1:2500)
F   third edition Ordnance Survey 1921 (1:2500)
G   after 1922

Where a facade has been added to a pre-existing building two letters are given, e.g. DB which signifies a facade of phase D on a building of phase B.

The second part of the entry gives a Roman numeral I-X for the style under which it has been grouped with a lower case letter showing the relevant section. Thus 42 Chester Street has the entry D ii X meaning that it appears on map D for the first time, is therefore to be dated 1835-1875, but is historically known to be late in that phase, 1855-75; it is described in Style X - miscellaneous.

An asterisk preceding the Roman numeral denoting the style shows that the building is illustrated in the plates, e.g. *IXa.

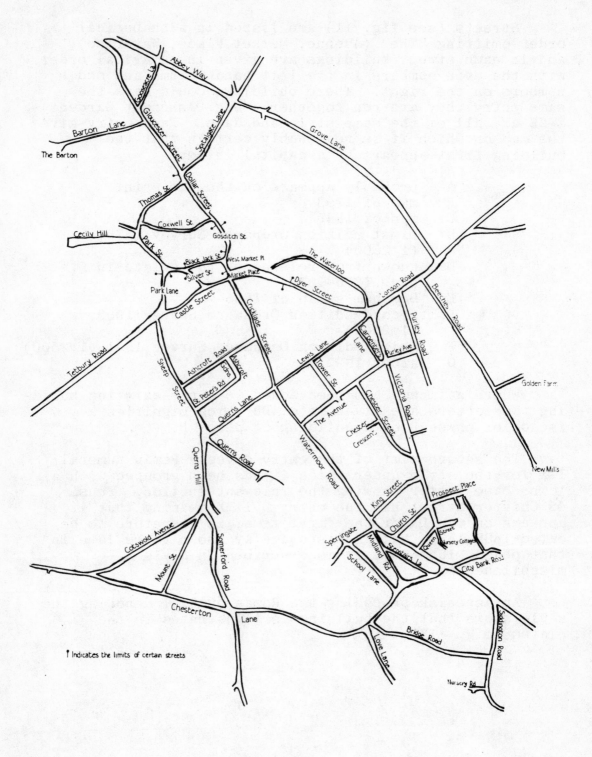

Fig. II

Cirencester: Street plan

Abbey Way

Ashcroft Gardens

2-22	Eii	IX(f)	1-11	F	IX(e)
24	Eii	IX(a)	15	Eii	VI(d)

Ashcroft Road

6	Eii	III(d)	1-9	Eii	IX(f)
28-40	Eii	IX(e)	Ashcroft Hall	Eii	IX(f)
42-46	Eii	IX(a)	11-17	Eii	IX(f)
48-54	Eii	VII(d)	19-21	Eii	IX(d)
56-58	Eii	VI(b)	Methodist Church	Eii	IX(f)
			Dairy	Eii	IX(f)
			27-33	Eii	IX(f)
			35-45	Eii	VI(a)
			47-61	Eii	VI(d)

Avenue

2 Leaholme	Ei	VI(b)	1-3	Eii	VII(c)
Masonic Hall	Eii	VII(d)	5-7	Dii	VIII(a)
4 + 6	Eii	VII(b)	9	Dii	VI(a)
8-12	Eii	VI(a)	15	G	III(d)
14-20	Dii	VI(b)	17	Dii	III(d)
22-24	Dii	III(d)	19-21	Ei	VI(d)
26-30	Eii	IX(f)			
32-34	Dii	VII(b)			
34a	Eii	III(d)			

Barton Lane

2 + 4	F	VII(a)
6-8	D	IV(d)
10-12	D	III(b)
14-16	G	
18 + 18(a)	1952	
20-22	1934	
24-26	1927	
28	D	IV(d)
30-32	G	
34-36	1946	
40 Mill House	B	VIII(a)
Barton Farm & farm buildings	A	*III(a)

Beeches Road

The Beeches	D	VI(a) VII(b)			
			1-19	C	IV(d)
Golden Farm	A	*I(c)	21-27	F	IX(f)
New Mills	A	III(a)	29	Eii	*X
			River Court		

Black Jack Street

2	D	*IX(b)	Crown		
2(a)	B	IV(b)	Garages	A	III(c)
2(b)	DB	VIII(b)	7	A	IV(a)
4	D	VI(b)	9-17	D	VII(c)
6	B	V(a)			
8	C	V(b)			
10	1909	VII(a)			
12	B	III(c)			
14-18	D	VI(a)			
20 Golden Cross	D	*X			
24-26	D	VI(b)			
28-38	D	X			
40-42	D	IX(e)			
44	D	III(d)			

Bridge Road

Gasworks	Ei	*IX(a)	1-17	F	IX(a)
Engine Sheds	Ei+F	VIII(d)			
Gas Offices	D	III(d)			
Gasworks Cottage	D	VI(a)			
Engine Sheds	1915+ Ei	IX(g)			

Carpenters Lane

Argyll House	Ei	VIII(c)	Furniture Store	Ei	VI(b)

Castle Street

2-12	1896/7	VII(c)	1	Ei	IX(a)
14 Lloyds Bank	B	*V(c)	3	B	III(b)
18	B	V(a)	5-7	D	VII(a)
20	D	VI(b)	9	Ei	VII(b)
22-26	A	I(d)	11	G	
28	Ei	VI(b)	15	A	I(c)
30	D	VII(c)	17	A	III(a)
32	E	VI(b)	19	A	*II
36	D	VI(b)	21	G	
38	1910	VII(c)	23	B	IV(b)
40	1858	VII(a)	25-29	1898	IX(d)
			31-33	C	V(c)
			35-37	D	VI(a)
			39	G	
			43	A	I(a)
			45	A	III(c)
			47	A	II
			51	F	IX(e)
			53	B	III(c)
			63	A	I(c)
			65-67		
			3 Compasses	F	VII(a)
			69-71	D	IV(d)

Cecily Hill

2	A	*I(d)	1	1880	VII(a)
4-28	1802	*V(a)	3	C	III(c)
32	B	*V(a)	5	BA	*V(a)
36	CB	VII(a)	7	A	V(b)
38	1909	VII(a)	9	A	*IV(a)
40 + 42	B	*V(a)	11-15	1777	*IV(d)
Militia Armoury	D	*VII(c)	17	D	VII(a)
46	D	VII(a)	19-25	C	*VII(a)
			27	A	I(a)
			29-31	D	VII(a)

Chester Crescent

2-22	Dii	VI(b)
24	F	IX(f)

Chester Street

2-14	Dii	VI(b)	1-21	Dii	VI(b)
16-20	Ei	VI(b)	25-75	Dii	VI(b)
22	Eii	VI(b)			
24-32	Ei	VI(b)			
34-40	Dii	VI(b)			
42	Dii	*X			
44-48	Dii	VI(a)			
50-54	Ei	VI(a)			
56-58	Dii	VI(a)			
60-62	Dii	III(d)			

Chesterton Lane

Cemetery Lodge	D	VII(c)	33-43	Eii	IX(c)
Cemetery			45	F	IX(d)
Chapels	D	VII(c)			
Chesterton Farm Lodge	C	VII(a)			
Chesterton House	C	V(a)			
Chesterton House Lodge	C	VI(b)			
54	D	VIII(c)			
56-72	D	III(d)			
74	Eii				
84-90	Eii	VIII(c)			

Church Street

2 + 4	Eii	III(d)	1	Dii	III(d)
6-26	Eii	*VIII(c)	1a	Dii	IX(c)
28	Dii	VI(a)	3	G	
30	Dii	III(d)	5-9	Eii	IX(e)
32	G		11-15	F	III(d)
34	Dii	IX(a)	17-23	Dii	VI(a)
36-40	Dii	III(d)	25-27	Dii	III(d)

City Bank Road

10	C	III(d)	1	D	III(d)

City Bank Road

14-16	A	III(a)	3	C	III(d)
			5-27	C	IX(f)
			27-43	F	IX(e)

Cotswold Avenue

Coxwell Street

2	1696	I(b)	1	1658	I(a)
6	CA	V(b)	3	A	I(c)
8 Jehova's			5	A	I(b)
Witness	E	VI(a)	25	1674	*I(a)
10	EA	*X	27-37	A	*III(a)
10(a)+(b)	E	VI(b)	Baptist		
12	D	VI(b)	Chapel	D	VI(a)
12(a)	B	IV(d)	39-43	C	V(a)
14-20	A	I(e)	45	C	*V(b)
22-28	B	VIII(a)	47 + 49	A	IV(a)
32 + 36	B	III(c)	51	A	*IV(a)
38 + 40	1882	VII(a)	53(a)	G	
			53	A	I(c)

Cricklade Street

2 + 4	E	VIII(b)	5 + 7	B	V(b)
6-6e	G		9	G	
10	D	IV(b)	11	DC	IX(a)
12	B	IV(b)	17	G	
14	DB	VI(a)	19-23	D	VI(a)
20	E	IX(b)	25	G	
26	G		31	D	VII(a)
28	G		33	D	IX(a)
30	E	VII(a)	39-41	C	III(d)
32-36	1893	VI(b)	43-65(a)	G	
38	F	IX(c)	67-71	F	IX(a)
40	F	VIII(b)	Wheatsheaf	B	I(c)
42	F	IX(a)	81	E	IX(a)
44	E	IX(e)	85	GC	
46	B	I(c)	89	C	III(c)
48-60	C	III(c)	91	C	IV(d)
62	B	III(d)	93-103	C	X
Malthouse	E	VI(b)	105-119	1935	
64 + 66	A	IV(a)	132-141	1889	VII(a)
68	F	IX(e)			
70 Brewers Arms	F	IX(a)			
72 + 74	B	I(d)			
76-82	C	IV(d)			

Dollar Street

2	D	*VII(a)	1 + 3	A	I(d)
4	A	I(e)	5	DA	VII(a)
6 + 8	A	II	7 + 9	C	V(c)
10 + 12	CA	V(b)	11-17	D	VI(c)
14	A	I(e)	19-27	G	
18	C	VII(a)			

Dollar Street

20	C	III(d)	29-41 Triangle	G	
22-28	D	VI(b)	43 + 45	C	*V(c)
30	B	*IV(b)	47 + 49	G	
32	B	*V(b)	51 + 53	D	VI(b)
34	D	VI(c)			
36	E	VIII(b)			
38	D	VI(d)			

Dugdale Road

14-16	C	III(b)

Dyer Street

2 + 4	A	I(c)	1	1904	VII(b)
6 + 8	D	VI(c)	3	C	V(b)
10	D	VI(b)	5	B	V(b)
12 The Bear	A	*II	7	B	V(a)
14-54 Forum	G		9-11	B	I(e)
56-58	DB	VI(b)	17	B	V(a)
60	BA	*V(b)	19	G	
60(a)	F	VI(b)	21	G	
62-66	D	VI(b)	25-27	G	
72	B	*IV(a)	29-31	E	VII(e)
74	E	VII(e)	33	C	V(c)
76-82	DC	VI(c)	35	B	VIII(b)
84 + 86	B	V(b)	37	E	III(d)
			39	A	I(c)
			41	A	III(d)
			43-45	D	VI(c)
			47-51	1889	VII(a)
			53-55	C	V(c)
			57	C	V(b)

Gloucester Street

2-6	A	*I(a)	1	G	
8	A	*IV(a)	3 + 5	1740	IV(a)
10	CB	IV(c)	7	A	*I(a)
12 + 14	CB	V(c)	19	A	I(b)
16-22	CB	IV(c)	25	C	VIII(a)
26	C	III(b)	27	D	*VI(b)
28	B	I(e)	29 Barton		
30	D	IV(d)	Hall	C	V(c)
40	A	I(b)	33 + 35	A	*II
48	D	VIII(b)	37-49	B	IV(d)
50 + 52	F	VIII(a)	51 + 53	A	I(e)
54	E	VII(b)	57	A	I(c)
56-60	C	III(c)	59-67	B	IV(d)
62-66	B	III(c)	83-89	C	IV(d)
Nelson			91 + 93	E	III(d)
Extension	B	III(c)	95 + 97	D	III(b)
70 Nelson	D	VI(b)	103	D	VI(b)
74	D	III(d)	105	1695	I(c)
76-80	D	VI(b)	107	C	V(b)

Gloucester Street

82-86	F	VII(a)	111-117	D	IV(d)
88-94	D+	III(a)	119	G	
96	A	II	141	A	II
98-100	B	III(c)	143	D	IV(d)
102-104			145-151	D	VI(b)
Royal Oak	D	III(c)	153-157	1906	VII(e)
106-112	D	IV(d)	169-177	A	III(a)
114-120	B	III(c)	185	D+	III(b)
122	F	VIII(b)	187	D+	VI(b)
			189-197	E	VIII(a)

Gosditch Street

Abbey House	G		1	C	VII(a)
Flats			3-5	B	*V(a)
			7-9	B	V(b)
			9(a)-11	C	V(b)
			15	1873	*VII(a)
			Unitarian		
			Church	1672	*I(a)
			17 + 19	A	II

Gooseacre Lane

2-4 Nelson			1-3	D	III(c)
Hall	F	III(c)	5	G	
6	G		7-9	F	IX(a)
8	G		11-15	A	I(b)
10	G		21	G	

Grove Lane

Saxon Arch	A	*Medieval
1	C	*VII(a)

King Street

2-24	F	VII(c)
Bingham Hall	F	VII(c)
28	F	VII(c)

Lewis Lane

2	F	VII(a)	1-7	1889	VII(a)
12 Twelve			9-21	C	VII(a)
Bells	DC	VI(c)	23-33	G	
14	A	I(e)	35-37	D	VI(b)
16	A	I(c)	39-41	D	VI(b)
18-30	D	VII(a)	45	G	
32-38	D	III(b)	Primitive Methodist		
40	G		Chapel	D	*IX(c)
Cinema	G		Telephone		
44-46	D	VI(a)	Exchange	G	
48	E	IX(d)	County Junior/		
50	E	IX(c)	Infants School	1879	VII(c)

Lewis Lane

52	D	VIII(a)	83	D	VI(b)
54 + 56	E	VIII(a)	85	C	IV(d)
			87	D	VI(b)

London Road

2-4	F	VIII(b)	5 + 7	C	V(b)
6-10	C	III(a)	9	D	VI(b)
12	F	IX(e)	11 Waggon &		
14	D	VII(a)	Horses	F	VII(a)
20 + 22	F	IX(e)	15	C	V(c)
26-28	F	VIII(a)	The Apple		
			Loft	E	*III(d)

Love Lane

Market Place

2	F	VII(d)	1	B	V(c)
			Parish Church	A	*Medieval
4-10	D	*IX(a)	3	C	V(c)
12-22	E	VI(a)	5 + 7	B	V(c)
Kings Head	D	*X	9-17	B	*IV(b)
Corn Hall	D	*X	19-23	B	V(a)
28-30	B	I(d)	25	B	V(b)
32	G		27	DB	VI(c)
34 + 36	D	VI(a)	29-33	C	V(b)
38 + 40	B	V(b)	35	A	III(a)
			37	B	V(a)
			39	D	VII(a)
			41 Fleece	A	*II
			43 Fleece	C	V(b)

Midland Road

Demolished without any record

Mount Street

2-6	Dii	VIII(c)	1-3	Eii	VI(b)
20	Dii	VIII(c)	5-17	Ei	VI(b)
			19-23	F	IX(e)
			25-39	F	IX(a)

Nursery Cottages

2-16	Eii	IX(e)

Nursery Road

2-8	F	IX(a)

Park Lane

Old Grammar			Cirencester		
School	A	I(c)	House	B	*V(a)

Park Lane

6	D	VI(a)
10-16	C	VII(a)

Park Street

2 + 4	A	I(c)	1-3	A	I(c)
6 + 8	C	V(a)	5 + 7	C	IV(d)
10	D	VI(a)	9	A	I(b)
12	B	V(a)	11	A	I(a)
14	C	V(a)	15	D	III(b)
			17	D	III(d)
			19	B	III(c)
			21	D	VI(a)
			23	E	VI(b)
			25	D	VI(a)
			Dunstall House	B	V(a)
			27	E	VI(b)
			29	C	V(b)

Prospect Place

2-20	Eii	III(d)	1-3	Ei	VI(b)
22-30	Eii	IX(e)	5	F	IX(e)
32-38	Eii	III(d)	7-15	Eii	IX(e)
			17	Eii	VIII(a)

Purley Avenue

2-4	F	IX(a)

Purley Road

2-56	F	IX(a)	1-17	F	IX(b)
			19-49	F	*IX(a)
			51-55	G	

Queen Street

2-4	Dii	III(d)	1-5	Ei	VI(b)
6	Dii	VI(b)	7-15	Dii	VI(b)
10 Forresters	E	VI(a)	17	Eii	VI(b)
12-22	Dii	VI(b)	19-37	Ei	IX(e)
24	Eii	IX(e)			
26-42	Ei	*IX(e)			

Querns Hill

			41	C	VIII(a)
			43-47	C	III(a)

Querns Lane

2-10	G		1	B	V(a)
14-36	G		3-17	C	*IV(d)

Querns Lane

38	F	IX(a)	19	C	*V(a)
40	G		21	D	VI(b)
42	G		23	C	III(a)
46	G		25	C	III(c)
54 The Hope	C	III(c)	29 + 31	G	
			33	G	
			35-39	C	V(a)

Querns Road

Wharfingers House	B	V(b)	Watermoor Hospital	C	*V(a)

St. Peters Road

2-16	F	*VIII(c)	1	Eii	IX(d)
18-36	Eii	VIII(c)	3-5	Eii	VIII(c)
			Presbytery	Eii	VII(c)
			St. Peters Church	Eii	VII(c)
			9-15	Eii	VIII(c)

School Lane

Demolished without any record

Sheep Street

Hospital Annexe	EC	VI(a)	The Marlborough	F	VII(b)
			3-15	D	VI(b)
			Hospital	1873	VII(e)
			23	C	IV(d)
			25	C	V(a)
			27	D	VI(b)
			29 + 31	A	I(c)
			33	G	
			35	C	III(c)

Siddington Road

Horse & Drill	C	III(d)
6 + 8	B	IV(b)
24-46	F	IX(a)

Silver Street

2	CB	V(a)	3	G	
4-6	B	IV(b)	5	D	VI(b)
8	F	VII(c)	7 + 9	D	IV(d)
10-14	D	VII(c)			

Somerford Road

2	Dii	VII(c)	49-51	Eii	IX(e)
4-10	Dii	VI(b)	Oakley Hall	Eii	VII(b)
12-14	Dii	VI(a)	Highfield		
16	A	III(c)	Cottage	Dii	III(d)
18	Dii	VI(d)	Highfield	Dii	VI(a)
20	Dii	VI(a)	Elm Grove	Dii	*VI(a)
22	Dii	VI(d)	East Cranhams	Dii	VI(a)
Laundry	F	IX(a)	Rooks Nest	Dii	VI(a)
30-36	F	VI(a)	Southleigh	Eii	VI(b)
38-40	Dii	VIII(a)	Magpies	F	III(d)

Sperringate

Watermoor School House	D	VII(a)
Watermoor School	D	VII(a)

Spitalgate Lane

2	B	III(c)	1	A	III(a)
			1(a) St. Johns Hospital	A	*Medieval
			3-9	1826	III(d)
			11-21	CB	IV(d)
			27	A	III(a)
			29	F	IX(c)

Stepstairs Lane

Demolished without any record

Tetbury Road

Toll House	A	III(a)	Kennels	1837	*VII(a)
Ammonite Cottage	E	*III(d)	Kennels Lodge	D	VII(a)
Upper Querns Lodge	C	VII(a)	Old Museum	D	VI(a)
Lower Querns Lodge	F	IX(a)			
Old Railway Station	D	VII(b)			
Oakley Cottage	D	VII(a)			
The Querns	C	*VII(b)			

Thomas Street

2	B	IV(d)	1	GB	
4 Weavers Hall	A	*Medieval	3-17	GB	
6	A	*I(d)	19-23	D	
8	B	*IV(c)	25	C	IV(d)

Thomas Street

10 Temperance Hall	D	VII(a)	27-37	C	III(a)	
12-16	C	V(c)	47	B	III(c)	
18	E	V(c)	49 + 51	C	V(a)	
20 + 22	C	*V(b)	53 Friends Meeting House	A	IV(c)	
24	D	VI(a)	Meeting House Porch	D	VI(a)	
26	A	Medieval	55-63 Triangle	G		
28	A	*Medieval	65	1882	VII(a)	
Little Mead	C	*IV(d)				

Tower Street

2-10	Dii	VI(b)	Jefferies	Dii	III(d)
12-16	Dii	III(d)			
18-22	Ei	VI(b)			
24-26	Ei	VI(d)			
28	Ei	IX(d)			
30-34	Dii	*IX(d)			

Victoria Road

2	Dii	VIII(c)	3	G	
4	Ei	VI(d)	5-9	F	VIII(c)
6	Dii	VI(d)	11	G	
6a	G		17	F	IX(e)
8-10	Dii	VII(c)	19-21	F	IX(f)
10a	Eii		Garages	G	
12	Eii	VI(d)	27-29	G	
Talbot	Dii	VIII(d)	31-33	G	
16	Dii	VI(a)	35-37	F	VI(a)
18-24	Dii	VI(b)	37a	G	
26-32	Ei	VIII(c)	39	F	VI(a)
Flats	G		41-49	F	VIII(c)
32a + b	G		51-67	F	IX(f)
34-40	Dii	VI(a)	69-73	Eii	IX(e)
42	Eii	VIII(c)	73a	G	
44-52	Dii	*VI(a)	75	Eii	VIII(c)
54	Ei	VI(a)	75a	G	VIII(c)
56-60	Eii	VI(d)	77-81	F	VIII(c)
62	G		83-89	1906	*IX(c)
Stonewalls	Dii	VII(c)	91	Eii	VI(d)
74-78	G		93	G	
80-82	Dii	VI(b)	95	Ei	VI(a)
84 Coop	Dii	IX(a)	Grammar School	1880	*VII(c)
86-96	Dii	III(d)	97	Eii	*VI(d)
98-100	Dii	VI(a)	99-101	1880	VIII(c)
102	Dii	VI(b)	101a	G	
			103-125	Eii	IX(e)

Waterloo

14 + 16	C	III(c)	15	D	VI(a)
			17-23	D	*X

Watermoor Road

2 Chesterton				1 Coles		
Manor	A	I(a) IV(c)		Mill	C	IV(d)
4-14	G	VII(a)		3	C	VII(a)
16-26	D	VI(a)		5-21	1826	*VII(a)
28	D	III(d)		23-25	F	VII(a)
Old Parsonage	D	VI(b)		27-29	F	VI(b)
Parsonage	D	VII(c)		31-41	E	VI(a)
Watermoor				Watermoor		
Church	D	VII(c)		House	C	V(c)
Queens Head				63-73	F	VII(c)
Garage	D	III(c)		75	D	VI(b)
Queens Head				77	D	VII(a)
New	D	VIII(d)		83-87	Ei	VI(b)
Queens Head				89-93	D	VI(b)
Old	C	III(d)		95	Eii	III(d)
38-42	C	III(d)		97-103	Eii	*VIII(b)
44-48	D	III(d)		105	Eii	IX(a)
50-52	D	VI(b)		107	Eii	
54-58	D	III(d)		109-119	Eii	IX(f)
64-76	D	III(d)		Plume &		
Hopes Foundry	E	VII(a)		Feathers	F	IX(d)
80-116	E	IX(e)		135-143	D	III(d)
				145-157	C	V(a)
				159	D	IX(a)
				161-165	Ei	IX(a)

West Market Place

2 + 4	B	V(c)		1	D	*X
				3(a)	B	V(b)
				5 + 7	B	V(c)
				11 Crown	B	V(a)
				13 Crown	DB	X
				15 Crown	CB	IX(a)
				21-25	D	*VI(a)

PLATE I

St. John's Hospital

Spitalgate Lane

Med.

The Saxon Arch

from the west

Med.

Parish Church Porch

from the south-west

Med.

Parish Church Tower

from the north-east

Med.

Weavers' Hall
4
Thomas Street

Med.

The Park, The Mansion

and the Church

from the west

Medieval and later

Stable Cottages

Barton Complex

I

Tythe Barn

Barton Complex

Med.

Monmouth House

28

Thomas Street

Med.

PLATE II

The Bear

12

Dyer Street

The Fleece

41

Market Place

19

Castle Street

33-35

Gloucester Street

II

Golden Farm

Beeches Road

Ic

7

Gloucester Street

Ia

25

Coxwell Street

Ia

Unitarian Church

Gosditch Street

Ia

19

Querns Lane

Va

8

Thomas Street

IVc

PLATE III

9
Cecily Hill
IVa

Little Bull
72
Dyer Street
IVa

White Lion
8
Gloucester Street
IVa

9-17
Market Place
from the North
IVb

2
Cecily Hill

Id

6
Thomas Street
Id

30
Dollar Street
IVb

5
Gosditch Street
Va

11-15
Cecily Hill
IVd

3-5
Querns Lane
IVd

PLATE IV

Lloyd's Bank

14

Castle Street

Vc

40-42

Cecily Hill

Va

32

Cecily Hill

Va

32

Dollar Street

Vb

20

Thomas Street

Vb

60

Dyer Street

Vb

45

Coxwell Street

Vb

43-45

Dollar Street

Vc

Watermoor Hospital

Querns Road

Va

4-28

Cecily Hill

Va

PLATE V

27-37	Old Apple Loft	Ammonite Cottage
Coxwell Street	London Road	Tetbury Road
IIIa	IIId	IIId

Tythe Barn	145-147
Barton Complex	Watermoor Road
IIIa	Va

97-103	6-26
Watermoor Road	Church Street
VIIIb	VIIIc

2-8	The Talbot
	14
St. Peter's Road	Victoria Road
VIIIc	VIIId

PLATE VI

Shadow of Timber

frame on   The Hexagon   5

27   The Park

Gloucester Street   Cecily Hill

II   IV   Va

Saxon Arch

and cottage   Little Mead

from the south   Thomas Street

VIIa   IVd

21-25   44-50

West Market Place Victoria Road

VIa   VIa

Elm Grove   97

Somerford Road   Victoria Road

VIa   VId

PLATE VII

2-4
Gloucester Street
Ia

5-21
Watermoor Road
VIIa

2
Dollar Street
VIIa

15
Gosditch Street
VIIa

19
Cecily Hill
VIIa

The Querns
Tetbury Road
VIIb

The Kennels
Tetbury Road
VIIa

The Armoury
Cecily Hill
VIIc

The Grammar School
Victoria Road
VIIc

PLATE VIII

Primitive Methodist

Chapel

Lewis Lane

IXc

30-34

Tower Street

IXd

4

Market Place

IXa

8

Market Place

IXa

2

Black Jack Street

IXb

26-42

Queen Street

IXe

Old Gas Works

Bridge Road

IXa

83-89

Victoria Road

IXe

23-29

Purley Road

IXa

PLATE IX

10	51	42
Coxwell Street	Coxwell Street	Chester Street
Xa	IVa	Xe

19	1	Golden Cross
Waterloo	West Market Place	Black Jack Street
Xb	Xc	Xc

Corn Hall	River Court	Kings Head
	29	
Market Place	Beeches Road	Market Place
Xd	Xd	Xd

British Archaeological Reports

122 Banbury Road, Oxford OX2 7BP, England

List of Titles

(Cheques & money orders should be made payable
to 'British Archaeological Reports' and sent to the
above address. Prices include postage.)

B.A.R. 1, 1974, "Cuddesdon and Dorchester-on-Thames, Oxford-
shire: two early Saxon 'princely' sites in Wessex", by
Tania M. Dickinson: 54 pp., 4 figs., 4 plates. Price
£0.75 ($2.20) post free.

B.A.R. 2, 1974, "The Deserted Medieval Village of Broad-
field, Herts," by Eric C. Klingelhöfer: 73 pp., 22 figs.,
1 plate. Price £0.80 ($2.30) post free.

B.A.R. 3, 1974, "A Corpus of Early Bronze Age Dagger Pommels
from Great Britain and Ireland", by Ron Hardaker: 65 pp.,
7 figs., 2 plates. Price £0.80 ($2.30) post free.

B.A.R. 5, 1974, "Some Iron Age Mediterranean Imports in England", by Peter Harbison and Lloyd R. Laing: 39 pp., 4
plates. Price £0.80 ($2.30) post free.

B.A.R. 6, 1974, "Anglo-Saxon Settlement and Landscape", ed.
Trevor Rowley: 138 pp., 15 figs., 7 plates. Price £2.00
($5.50) post free.

B.A.R. 7, 1974, "A Corpus of Pagan Anglo-Saxon Spear-Types",
by M.J. Swanton: 90 pp., 4 figs. Price £1.10 ($3.00) post
free.

B.A.R. 8, 1974, "A Corpus of Roman Engraved Gemstones from
British Sites", by Martin Henig: Part i, Discussion, 205 pp.,
4 figs.; Part ii, Catalogue and Plates, 117 pp., 61 plates.
Price (parts i and ii together) £5.00 ($12.00) post free.

B.A.R. 9, 1974, "Grooved Ware Sites in Yorkshire and the North
of England", by T.G. Manby: 133 pp., 43 figs., 2 plates.
Price £2.00 ($5.50) post free.

B.A.R. 10, 1975, "Stamp and Roulette Decorated Pottery of the
La Tène Period in Eastern England: a Study in Geometric
Designs", by Sheila M. Elsdon: 115 pp., 19 figs., 5 plates.
Price £2.30 ($6.00) post free.

B.A.R. 12, 1975, "Cirencester: the Development and Build-
ings of a Cotswold Town", by Richard Reece and Christopher
Catling: 78 pp., frontispiece and 11 figs., 9 plates.
Price £1.50 ($4.00) post free.

B.A.R. 13, 1975, "Settlement Types in Post-Roman Scotland",
by Lloyd R. Laing: 46 pp., 25 figs. Price: £1.00 ($2.60)
post free.

B.A.R. 14, 1975, "Clay Pipes for the Archaeologist", by
Adrian Oswald: 207 pp., 23 figs., 6 plates. Price £3.80
($10.00) post free.